通用英语听说教程

- 主　编　许　敏
- 副主编　李　建
- 编　委　杨可炜　刘　玲

苏州大学出版社
Soochow University Press

图书在版编目(CIP)数据

通用英语听说教程/许敏主编. —苏州:苏州大学出版社,2015.12(2021.1重印)
ISBN 978-7-5672-1606-8

Ⅰ.①通… Ⅱ.①许… Ⅲ.①英语－听说教学－高等学校－教材 Ⅳ.①H319.9

中国版本图书馆CIP数据核字(2015)第306067号

本书录音下载:www.sudapress.com/down.asp.

书　　名:	通用英语听说教程
主　　编:	许　敏
责任编辑:	杨　华
封面设计:	刘　俊
出版发行:	苏州大学出版社(Soochow University Press)
社　　址:	苏州市十梓街1号 邮编:215006
印　　刷:	苏州工业园区美柯乐制版印务有限责任公司(电话号码0512-67606001)
网　　址:	www.sudapress.com
邮购热线:	0512-67480030
销售热线:	0512-65225020
开　　本:	787×1092 1/16 印张:16.75 字数:397千
版　　次:	2015年12月第1版
印　　次:	2021年1月第5次印刷
书　　号:	ISBN 978-7-5672-1606-8
定　　价:	45.00元

凡购本社图书发现印装错误,请与本社联系调换。服务热线:0512-67481020

前 言

《通用英语听说教程》依据教育部颁布的《大学英语课程教学要求》设计和编写，广泛借鉴了国内外优秀英语教材的编写经验，旨在通过国际化的资源和视野、多角度的思维方式和实用的学习方法，提升学生在真实场景与多元文化中的英语听说交流能力，培养具有人文素养、科学素养和学术能力的全面发展的人才。

《通用英语听说教程》包括15个单元。每单元的设计思路是：以简单轻松的词汇引入单元主题，激发学生兴趣，调动学生进一步深入了解和探讨主题的积极性，为接下来的学习任务做好准备。之后的相关词汇、相关句型都围绕这一主题展开，对于主题的不同视角、观点或相互补充，或截然相反，引导学生多角度、多层次地看待问题，注重培养学生口头实用表达能力。学生在对话题充分理解和自由讨论后将阅读一两篇和话题有关的短文，进行与主题相关的思辨训练如课堂辩论及研讨，进一步加深对这类话题的理解，提升思辨类话题的口语表达能力。教材中与主题相关的听力材料内容丰富，练习多样；听力材料涉及许多热议话题，具有较强的思辨性和启发性，为后续口语活动做好语言及观点准备。在大量的语言和信息输入之后，单元最后的Assignment既可以作为课堂练习，也可以作为学生的自主学习内容，要求学生综合运用单元所学的内容和听说技巧，独立完成或合作完成具有一定难度的综合任务。每个单元所有内容都围绕一个主题，编排与主题相关的口语活动，环环相扣，有机融合，为学生创造表达观点、锻炼思维、培养口语能力的氛围。每三个单元后安排了一个复习单元，将前面单元里出现的话题汇总，补充一些听力和口语的练习供学生及时巩固复习，并集中补充了一些口语技能讲解和配套练习以满足程度较高学生的需求。

本教材的编写团队为许敏、李建、杨可炜、刘玲。编者衷心感谢苏州大学出版社为本教材的出版给予的支持。对本教材所选用的网络资源，编者在此致以深切的谢意。本教材的编写从内容到形式都有不少新的尝试，由于编者水平有限，书中的错误或不妥之处在所难免，敬请读者批评指正。

编 者
2015年12月

CONTENTS

✤ Module 1　Campus　/1

1.1　Listening and speaking　/2
- 1.1.1　Asking for directions　/2
- 1.1.2　Campus life　/3
- 1.1.3　On-campus recreation　/7
- 1.1.4　Living on campus　/8

1.2　Critical thinking and speaking　/9
- Task 1　Living on campus vs. off campus　/9
- Task 2　Why go to college?　/11

Assignment　/12

✤ Module 2　Transportation　/16

2.1　Listening and speaking　/17
- 2.1.1　Short-distance transportation　/17
- 2.1.2　Long-distance transportation　/25

2.2　Critical thinking and speaking　/28
- Task 1　Internet transforms the way people hail a taxi　/28
- Task 2　Car-booking apps start moving up the ladder　/32

Assignment　/34

✤ Module 3　Telecommunications　/36

3.1　Listening and speaking　/37
- 3.1.1　Development of telecommunications　/37
- 3.1.2　Telephone skills　/40
- 3.1.3　Internet addiction　/46
- 3.1.4　Information security　/48

3.2　Critical thinking and speaking　/49
- Task 1　Social networking services in America　/49
- Task 2　Social networking services（SNS）　/50
- Task 3　Social networking sites: Friend or foe?　/51

Assignment　/54

✤ Module 4　Review　/56

4.1　Note-taking skills　/57

      4.1.1   The Cornell Method　　/57
      4.1.2   Note-taking practice　　/62
  4.2   Further listening and speaking　　/63
      4.2.1   Taped library tour　　/63
      4.2.2   Traffic ticket　　/65
      4.2.3   Smart phones　　/67
  4.3   Communication bank　　/70

✿ Module 5　Travel　/72

  5.1   Listening and speaking　　/73
      5.1.1 Deciding where to go　　/73
      5.1.2 Package tour vs independent travel　　/75
      5.1.3 Reserving a hotel room　　/77
      5.1.4 Booking a flight　　/78
      5.1.5 Holiday travel　　/79
      5.1.6 At the airport　　/82
  5.2   Critical thinking and speaking　　/83
      Task 1　Rubbish island　　/83
      Task 2　Space tourism　　/85
Assignment　/86

✿ Module 6　Leisure Activities　/88

  6.1   Listening and speaking　　/89
      6.1.1　Deciding what to do　　/89
      6.1.2　Amusement park　　/91
      6.1.3　Extreme sports　　/93
  6.2   Critical thinking and speaking　　/96
      Task 1　Extreme sports in South Africa　　/96
      Task 2　Balancing work and leisure　　/97
Assignment　/99

✿ Module 7　Food　/102

  7.1   Listening and speaking　　/103
      7.1.1　Deciding what to eat　　/103
      7.1.2　Making a reservation in a restaurant　　/104
      7.1.3　Reading a restaurant menu　　/105
      7.1.4　Asking about dishes on a menu　　/107
      7.1.5　Ordering a meal in a restaurant　　/108
      7.1.6　Food review　　/112
      7.1.7　Rising and falling intonations　　/114

7.2　Critical thinking and speaking　/115
　　Task 1　Healthy food or junk food?　/115
　　Task 2　Shall we say "no" to junk food?　/119
Assignment　/120

Module 8　Review　/122

8.1　Group discussion skills　/123
　　8.1.1　Group discussion & its skills　/123
　　8.1.2　Group discussion practice　/129
8.2　Further listening and speaking　/131
　　8.2.1　Travel peak: Chinese National Day　/131
　　8.2.2　Health benefits of having hobbies and leisure activities　/133
　　8.2.3　Where to serve the dishes on a table　/135
8.3　Communication bank　/137

Module 9　Job and Career　/139

9.1　Listening and speaking　/140
　　9.1.1　Career terms　/140
　　9.1.2　Career search　/141
　　9.1.3　Finding a job　/142
　　9.1.4　Advice on campus life　/143
　　9.1.5　How to talk about your job　/144
　　9.1.6　Do you feel boxed in?　/145
　　9.1.7　Office party　/146
9.2　Critical thinking and speaking　/147
　　Task 1　Do you "work to live or live to work"?　/147
　　Task 2　Differences between job and career　/148
Assignment　/150

Module 10　Volunteer　/152

10.1　Listening and speaking　/153
　　10.1.1　Volunteer organization　/153
　　10.1.2　International Volunteer Day　/155
　　10.1.3　Volunteering helps you live longer　/158
　　10.1.4　What are the best reasons to volunteer?　/162
　　10.1.5　Types of volunteer organizations　/164
　　10.1.6　Where to volunteer your time　/165
10.2　Critical thinking and speaking　/166
　　Task 1　How to volunteer: 10 steps to follow　/166

Task 2   UNNC students set to spend summer volunteering in rural areas   /170

Assignment   /171

✦ Module 11   Health   /173

11.1   Listening and speaking   /174
- 11.1.1   Describing your ailments   /174
- 11.1.2   A visit to the doctor's   /175
- 11.1.3   Top 5 myths about mental health   /180
- 11.1.4   Superbugs   /181

11.2   Critical thinking and speaking   /182
Task 1   Nutrition facts label   /182
Task 2   Health and fitness   /185

Assignment   /187

✦ Module 12   REVIEW   /189

12.1   Presentation skills   /190
- 12.1.1   Skills to improve presentation   /190
- 12.1.2   Informative impromptu speech practice   /195

12.2   Further listening and speaking   /197
- 12.2.1   Career search   /197
- 12.2.2   Volunteer work   /198
- 12.2.3   A healthy lifestyle   /200

12.3   Communication bank   /202

✦ Module 13   Men and Women   /204

13.1   Listening and speaking   /205
- 13.1.1   Differences between men and women   /205
- 13.1.2   Physical differences between men and women   /208
- 13.1.3   Non-physical differences between men and women   /209
- 13.1.4   Gender equality   /211

13.2   Critical thinking and speaking   /213
Task 1   Sayings quiz: Men and women   /213
Task 2   Gender roles   /214
Task 3   How acceptable do you think each of the following is?   /216
Task 4   Top 5 qualities women look for in a man   /217

Assignment   /218

✦ Module 14   City Life   /220

14.1   Listening and speaking   /221

14.1.1　The city and the country　/221
14.1.2　A super city—good or bad?　/224
14.1.3　Urban lifestyle choice　/225
14.1.4　City living makes it harder to concentrate　/227
14.1.5　Traffic in cities　/229

14.2　Critical thinking and speaking　/230
Task 1　Walking faster than ever　/230
Task 2　Top 10 livable cities in China in 2013　/235

Assignment　/239

Module 15　Future　/241

15.1　Listening and speaking　/242
15.1.1　The future of the human race　/242
15.1.2　Future science and technology　/246
15.1.3　Future telling　/247
15.1.4　Future planning　/250

15.2　Critical thinking and speaking　/252
Task 1　Studying the future　/252
Task 2　Would you take a one-way trip to the Mars?　/253

Assignment　/254

Module 1　Campus

Are you familiar with your campus?

Where can you find places to eat?

Where can you enjoy sports with your friends?

What kind of extracurricular activities are available on campus?

What shall we consider when deciding whether to live on campus or off campus?

...

1.1 Listening and speaking

1.1.1 Asking for directions

🔊 *Listen to the dialogue and try to fill in the blanks with proper phrases provided below.*

> got in touch / on top of that / opposite direction / Go straight down / left hand side

I went to Vancouver for a meeting this week. I have always liked Vancouver, and （1）_____ , my cousin Dominick just moved there. I （2）_____ with him and he invited me over to see his new place. On the way over, though, I got a little lost. I knew I was in the right area, but I was turned around. He lived in an apartment over an old bakery and I couldn't find it. I stopped a man who was walking by to ask for directions.

Lucy: Excuse me, could you tell me how to get to the Cross Bakery building?

Man: The Cross Bakery building? Oh, sure. You're actually walking in the （3）_____.

Lucy: Oh, you're kidding! I thought I was heading east.

Man: No, east is the other direction. To get to the Bakery, you need to turn around and go three blocks to Broadway. When you get to the intersection of Broadway and Elm, you hang left. （4）_____ that street for half a block and then you'll see the building on your left.

Lucy: Okay, let me see if I've got that. I need to go down Elm until I hit Broadway, then I make a left and the building is on my （5）_____. Is that right?

Man: Yeah, you've got it. Do you want me to show you the way?

Lucy: Thanks for the offer, but I think I've got it. Hopefully, I won't get lost again on my way there!

Useful expressions

Asking for directions	Showing the way
• How can I get to …?	• Then take a left/ turn left/make a left.
• Where does this street lead to?	• It's two-lane traffic.
• Which is the way to …?	• You will see a supermarket on your left.
• Is this the right way to the Red Rose Hotel?	• The post office is just right across the street.
• Can you tell me how to get to …?	• Make a right, pass two stop signs and you will
• Am I going in the right direction to …?	run into a supermarket.

1.1.2 Campus life

Campus life is colorful and full of fun. Campus life can be very colorful with various student activities and exciting parties, but can be very stressful as well, for study and love don't always go as well as one expected.

🔊 **1. Listen to the dialogue. Find out the incorrect information and then correct them.**

> ➢ The man fell in love with the girl in the dialogue.
>
> ➢ The man needed help on study.
>
> ➢ The girl in the dialogue gave no advice to the man.
>
> ➢ The man met the girl he liked in the library.

🔊 **2. Listen to the dialogue and write the missing phrases.**

（1）Sure. I am ready to_____ anybody. I went in for soccer when I was in high school.

（2）_____. Let's go to the field.

（3）You _____ lose the game to me, right?

（4）You must be joking! Don't be too hopeful! I'm _____.

3. Match the English college terms (1-12) with the corresponding English definitions.

Terms	Definitions
(1) Dean	A. The total number of points per credit hour earned（A=4, B=3,C=2, D=1, F=0）divided by college-level credit hours attempted.
(2) Semester	B. An administrator in charge of a division of a university or college. BHC has deans in the following areas: Instruction and Academic Support, Student Support Services and Instruction, and Student Learning.
(3) Grade Point Average（GPA）	C. A concentration of courses in a specific educational area.
(4) Elective	D. Various types of financial help including scholarships, work-study jobs or grants to eligible students.
(5) Syllabus	E. The period of time in which courses are scheduled. The summer session is either a four-week or eight-week session. Also referred to as a term.
(6) Tuition	F. Courses a student takes through the Internet.
(7) Major	G. Classes you choose to take that are not specifically required for graduation, but will increase your knowledge and help meet the remaining credit hours for a college degree.
(8) Financial aid	H. A document that lists a course's objectives and requirements. Each instructor distributes it at the beginning of the semester.
(9) Online courses	I. The official at most colleges and universities who is responsible for maintaining student records.
(10) Registrar	J. The cost of college classes based on the student's Residence and how many credits the student enrolls in for any given semester. Additional fees may apply.
(11) Credit hours	K. A way to teach courses to several sites at a time by means of the interactive television system.
(12) Distance learning	L. The amount of credits a student receives for completing a specific course. They are based upon the number of hours a class meets per week that are then equated to college credits.

Module 1 Campus

Tips

A compound noun is made up of two words, e.g. skydiving, ice-skating.

- In a compound noun, the main stress is usually on the first word.
- The second word has a lighter stress.

Repeat these compound nouns.

- bike riding
- skydiving
- scuba-diving
- ice-skating
- hang-gliding
- horseback riding
- ice cream
- eye doctor

- music activity
- publications school
- sponsored activity
- academic enrichment activity
- leadership employment
- work experience
- athletic activity
- community service
- activity beyond school
- religion

Group work

Discussion

Work in groups. Make a list of after-class activities on campus and report to your classmates.

5

- Music Activities
- Publications School
- Sponsored Activities
- Academic Enrichment Activities
- Leadership Employment
- Work Experience
- Athletic Activities
- Community Service
- Activities Beyond School
- Religion

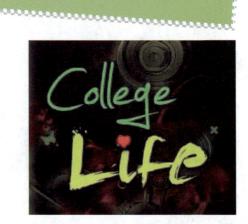

Module 1   Campus

1.1.3 On-campus recreation

🔊 Ben and Mark are students at University of Georgia (UGA). They are reading a brochure about on-campus recreation and trying to decide what to do this term. Listen to their talk and take down notes while listening.

Athletic options	Non-athletic options

Word tips

aikido	a Japanese martial art employing principles similar to judo
freshman fifteen	the fifteen pounds that students often gain during their first year of college in America
athletic	physically strong and good at sports
yearbook	a book printed every year by a school which contains class pictures of every student and information about all the clubs
DJ	disc jockey; the person who plays the songs on the radio
that sucks	(very informal) that's not good
check ... out	get information about something

Pair work

Work in pairs. Discuss with your partner about the following questions and take notes while listening. Then report to the class later.

- What do students like to do for on-campus recreation?
- What are the benefits of on-campus recreation?

7

1.1.4 Living on campus

- On campus – Residence Halls/Dorms
- Off campus
  - At home
  - Student-oriented apartment complexes
  - Other apartments or houses

What should be paid attention when living on campus?
- safety
- relationship
- time management
- money management

Ask yourself the following questions about self-regulation:
- When to go to bed? When to wake up?
- When and what to eat?
- When to come home? Whether to come home?
- How often to shower? How clean to keep your room?
- How much money to spend? What to spend money on?

Cultural notes

If you choose to live on campus, the following skills are necessary.
- Independent Living Skills

— Personal Hygiene	— Safety	— Transportation
— Health/First-Aid	— Nutrition	— Communication
— Money Management	— Housekeeping/Cleaning	

Group work

What else can you add up to the list above? Discuss with your group members and share with the class later.

1.2 Critical thinking and speaking

Task 1

Living on campus vs. off campus

It's the question that every college student must answer: Should you live on campus or off campus? Both options have their advantages and disadvantages, so it is crucial for you to weigh your choices before you make a final decision. To help you choose between the two, here are some pros and cons of both. Read the passage below and summarize the pros and cons in key words and fill in the blanks in the table.

on campus		off campus	
pros	cons	pros	cons

On campus

Pros
- Accessibility to the school. If you live on campus, you can easily walk to classes, libraries, computer labs, cafeterias, etc. You don't have to waste time and money on driving to school, finding a parking space, and so forth.
- Increased social life. Living on campus will allow you to meet more people and establish more friendships than if you live off campus. Living in a dorm means that there will always be someone around to hang out with. You will also usually be aware of any campus activities and how to be involved in them.
- Simplicity. If you live on campus, you don't have to worry about monthly rent payments, utility bills, and grocery shopping. Most students who live in a dorm get a meal plan in order to make eating easy and convenient.

Cons
- Little privacy. When living in a dorm, it can be very hard to find privacy. You have to share bedrooms, bathrooms, etc. The close living quarters mean that you may never have quiet time in your dorm because there will always be something going on.
- Limited space. At most colleges, the dorm rooms are tiny. You have to limit what you bring to school, or your space will be too crowded. That means you can't bring a different pair of shoes for every outfit.
- Possible low GPA. Because dorm life is very social, your grades may be affected in a negative way. If you constantly choose hanging out with your dorm buddies over studying at the library, then your GPA will suffer.

Off campus

Pros
- Independence. You will not have to follow as many rules if you live off campus. Residence halls have several rules that students must abide by when living on campus.（These rules are usually designed for the overall protection and safety of the residents.）Living off campus will give you freedom from those rules and allow you to set your own.
- Privacy. Living off campus means that you will more than likely have your own bedroom so you can have a place to sneak off and have time alone away from your roommates. The extra space also means that you can probably find a quiet place to study in the convenience of your own home.
- Sense of responsibility. Living off campus will help you be more responsible. If you live off campus, you will be in charge of paying bills, cleaning house, grocery shopping, and cooking. Being responsible is a good quality to possess（in case you consider this one a con）.

Cons
- More expensive. Often times, off-campus housing is more expensive than on-campus housing. Utilities and cable can be an added monthly expense, and you may have to pay for your own Internet access. You will also need to buy furniture, kitchen essentials, bath necessities, cleaning supplies, etc., which can be a hefty start-up cost.
- Transportation. When living off campus, it may not be convenient for you to walk to campus so you would have to find transportation. Whether you drive your car or use a form of public transportation, it is still going to cost you money. Traffic can also be an issue if you live in a crowded area.
- Isolation. If you live off campus, you may not be as involved with campus activities as you would if you live on campus. This could cause you to feel a sense of detachment with your college.

Task 2

Why go to college?

Ask your partner the question, "Why do you go to college?" Collect their answers and exchange the information with the rest of the class.

Why go to college?

With all of the talk that a student must hear about getting ready for college, some students may raise the pertinent question, "Why go to college in the first place?" It is a very important question that has different answers for different people. The three main reasons for attending college are increased pay, higher education, and the college experience. Some students will go to college for one, two, or all of these reasons. It really depends on the individual.

First is higher pay. Studies have shown that a person with a college degree will make about 80 percent more than a person with just a high school degree. That is almost twice as much. For example, the average high school graduate without any college education makes around $37,000. The average college graduate makes around $66,000. Of course, this is just the average. Some graduates will make less, and others will make much more. There is no guarantee that a college graduate will obtain a high-paying job. On the other hand, nothing says that a person with only a high school degree cannot make a very good living and be satisfied with his or her career. Odds are, however, if you want to make more money at your future job, going to college is the practical choice.

The next reason is that most students will go to college. This reason is to attend a place of higher learning. For students wanting to further their education, college is the next logical step. Many students will have a certain career in mind, and they need to go to school to get the education they need for that career. Other students do not know what they want to do with their life, but they are pretty sure they will find the answer in college. Taking a variety of classes at the college level can help a person decide on an avenue that they want to pursue.

Finally, there is the college experience. The college experience is a unique one that allows the individual to grow as a person. You are placed into a world that is much bigger than one you have previously experienced. You meet new people from various backgrounds and learn more about yourself as well. College is a place where you can redefine yourself. You have a chance to pursue your own interests and learn about the interests of others.

These are just a few of the reasons that students choose to go to college. There are many others. The point is that attending college will open many doors for you. It is up to you to decide if the process is worth the effort. In most cases, it will be.

by **Kelley O'Connor**

Assignment

Work in groups. Investigate at least 10 college students by asking them to finish the following quiz. Then analyze the answers and report to the class next time. You can use the following passage as your reference when analyzing.

Stress quiz for college students

1. Your best friend fails on plans to help you with a class project. You _____.

   ☐ do your best work on your own

   ☐ burst into tears

   ☐ call anyone who owes you a favor

2. When you get into bed, you fall asleep _____.

   ☐ immediately

   ☐ after an hour or two

   ☐ after a few minutes

3. When was the last time you had a headache?

   ☐ Yesterday.

   ☐ Last week.

   ☐ A few months ago.

4. How do you feel before you take a really tough test?

   ☐ Confident.

   ☐ So nervous that you can't focus.

   ☐ Slightly anxious.

5. How do you manage balancing all your homework, after-school activities, and personal responsibilities?

   ☐ Keep a prioritized list.

   ☐ Try to do everything asap.

   ☐ Cut out all personal stuff.

6. When something does not go your way, you_____.

☐ get angry and take it out on others

☐ deal with it and move on

☐ blow off steam at the gym

7. Your significant bad habit is_____.

☐ listening to your iPad

☐ constantly biting your nails

☐ being late for class

8. Your day planner consists of_____.

☐ tons of random notes and to-do lists

☐ what day planner

☐ color-coded appointments and lists

9. How often do you make time to exercise or do some other de-stressing activities?_____

☐ Rarely.

☐ Sometimes.

☐ Often.

10 ways to manage college stress

1. **Manage yourself.** Most people talk about managing time in order to have more of what life has to offer, but it's only in managing ourselves that we really see a difference in our lives and are able to handle any stress life throws at us. Manage yourself and other things will fall into place.

2. **Control your environment by controlling who and what is surrounding you.** Life is like a teacup. There's only so much "stuff" that will fit into it. If you fill your cup with the wrong things and the wrong people, you won't have time for the right things and the right people. The wrong things and people bring stress. The right things and people bring joy and contentment. Choose who and what gets your time and attention.

3. **Be good to yourself.** Acknowledge yourself for the good you do! Be gentle with yourself when things don't go as you might have wanted them to. There are just some things that you can't control — no matter how much you want to. Love yourself for who you are right now — at this very moment.

4. **Reward yourself.** Leisure activities are otherwise known as recreational activities. When you do things that bring you joy, you are re-creating your spirit. Nurturing your spirit is a great way to help you reduce stress. Take time to do things that reward you, every day.

5. **Exercise your body.** Health and vitality depend on your body's ability to use oxygen and food effectively. One of the ways to help that happen is through exercise. Exercise also releases endorphins, which have been shown to improve one's mood, making it a great way to deal with stress! Move your body every day!

6. **Relax yourself.** What do you do to really relax? Do you even take the time, or know how to? Meditation, listening to soothing music, spending time with friends and people you love, conscious breathing … these are all ways to really relax. If your mind is pulled to the things that stress you, you aren't really relaxed! Take time to be absolutely quiet every day.

7. **Rest yourself.** It's important to take breaks. There's a reason why employers give you several breaks during the day. Take them. While you are responsible for your own study schedule, it's critical to your success that you take time to rest — away from your desk — take naps if you're feeling nappish! It's also important to get sufficient sleep. Most people need at least seven hours each night. Good sleep habits include having a set bed time and a set waking time. Did you know that if you don't get the amount of sleep you need, you can be off （in your ability to think, respond and judge） by as much as 50% the next day? Following a pattern and establishing a rhythm for yourself and your body help you be more relaxed and less stressed during the day. Go to bed! Don't apologize for wanting to "turn in" early!

8. **Be aware of yourself.** Pay attention to your body. It gives you clues as to what it needs, and when something is wrong with it. Also, know what makes you feel great, and what makes you feel lousy. Being able to recognize them will help you make great decisions for yourself. Also, listen to your intuition. Your wise self never gives you the wrong answers. Your head, on the other hand, will almost always try to talk you out of it. Wake up and pay attention. You learn all sorts of things this way!

9. **Feed yourself and avoid poisoning your body.** Our minds have really been polluted with ideas of what a "healthy" diet looks like, and what "proper" nutrition is. Learn about what things like "low fat" prepared foods, sugar, fat, caffeine and tap water are really doing to your body. Improper nutrition causes stress in the body. It's not hard to get the right information and make great choices for yourself. Eat good stuff!! Your body will thank you!

10. **Enjoy yourself.** We've all seen stories of people who are diagnosed with some horrible disease and given six months to live who have, in those last months, really developed a love of life — a desire to enjoy it all. Well, forget about the person with only 6 months …. What about you? You probably only have 80 or so years if even that … Shouldn't each moment of your life be utterly succulent too? There's only so much time in this life. Every moment of it is precious. Make it all count. When you do, you'll find you have less stress, fewer physical problems, and that you're more productive. Look for the good/sweet/fun/joyous in every situation, even when life seems less than fair.

Self-assessment

Review the content covered in this module. How well can you do each of the following?

	very well	well	not well
I know how to ask for directions.	○	○	○
I know how to talk about campus life.	○	○	○
I know how to describe my dormitory.	○	○	○
I know the differences between living on campus and off campus.	○	○	○

Module 2
Transportation

Whether you live on or off campus, you can't live without certain public or private transport. In this module, you will learn to:

- talk about different means of transportation;
- behave properly while talking public or private transportation;
- choose the appropriate transportation to get to your destination.

2.1 Listening and speaking

2.1.1 Short-distance transportation

1. Work alone to match the following words with the letters A-L.

bicycle	_____	airplane	_____	subway	_____	cab	_____
car	_____	train	_____	segway	_____	hitch-hiking	_____
scooter	_____	motorbike	_____	coach	_____	ship	_____

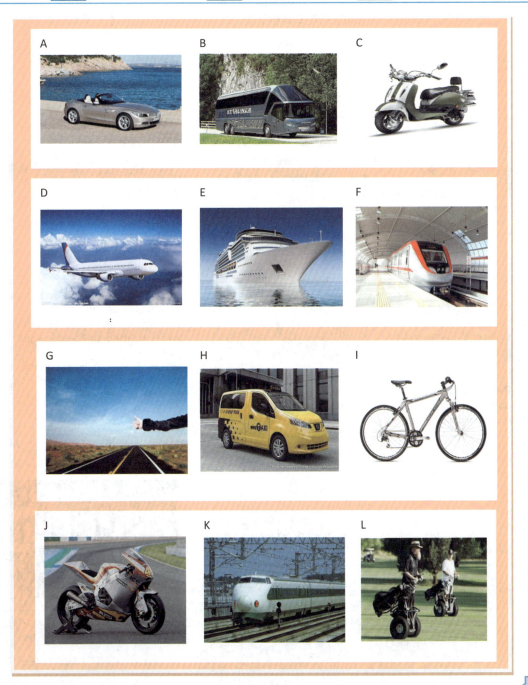

2. Listen to the passage and choose the correct answer to each of the following questions.

(1) What are the two main points Randall explains in the audio about cycling?
   A. Cost savings and healthy lifestyle.
   B. Proper attire and shoes.
   C. Riding gear and safety.

(2) A key point Randall mentions is that you should _____.
   A. know how to use your equipment before you ride
   B. buy the proper bike for your particular riding needs
   C. wear a safety vest while riding your bike

(3) What does Randall suggest about having lights for your bike?
   A. Buy red lights so people can see you better.
   B. Put lights on the front and back of your bike.
   C. Get blinking lights that attract drivers' attention.

Cultural notes — Bicycle-riding in the USA

Bicycle safety equipment:
Investment in safety equipment such as protective clothing and a **helmet** can prevent a significant number of injuries.
☆ Helmets are extremely important. Helmet use has been estimated to reduce head injury risk by 85%, according to the Insurance Institute for Highway Safety.
☆ Reflective clothing for night-time or low-visibility conditions.
☆ Bicycle **reflectors** on frame and wheels.
☆ Proper bicycle selection.
☆ Bicycle maintenance.

Bicycling safety guidelines:
Consideration of these tips can further reduce the risk of a bicycle accident.
☆ Use a bicycle only in a way that is appropriate for the age of the rider.
☆ Less experienced bicyclists should be educated about the rules of the road.
☆ Be aware of the understanding among bicyclists and motorists about sharing the road.
☆ Promote and ensure safe motorist and bicyclist practices (proper speed, yielding right-of-way, not driving or riding while under the influence of alcohol or drugs). In some states in the U.S., it is illegal to ride a bicycle under the influence of alcohol.
☆ Teach increased awareness of surroundings. (Beware of opening car doors, sewer **gratings**, **debris** on roads, uneven surfaces and poorly lit areas.)

Word tips

helmet: A hard hat that you wear to protect your head.
reflector: A small piece of plastic that is fastened to a bicycle or to a piece of clothing so that it can be seen more easily at night. All bikes sold in the UK must be fitted with reflectors.
grating: A metal frame with bars across it, used to cover a window or hole.
debris: Pieces of wood, metal, brick, etc. that are left after something has been destroyed.

3. Listen to the dialogue and fill in the blanks.

A: Hey, buddy, (1) _____ you see there's a line?
B: Oh, sorry. I didn't know.
A: What? You haven't (2) _____ the bus before?
B: No, I'm afraid not.
A: Well, you have to wait in line like everyone else. Besides, you should let (3) _____ on first.
B: Sorry.
A: It's all right. Where are you going?
B: I wanted to see the White House.
A: Oh, well, you don't want this bus, anyway. It goes to Georgetown.
B: Oh, no.
A: It's all right, though. Just get off at the next stop and catch the 79A.
B: Oh, well thank you very much.
A: You're welcome.

4. Work with your partner to find the substitutes for the underlined words or expressions.

A: Hey, buddy, (1) _____ you see there's a line?
B: Oh, sorry. I didn't know.
A: What? You haven't (2) _____ the bus before?
B: No, I'm afraid not.
A: Well, you have to wait in line like everyone else. Besides, you should let (3) _____ on first.
B: Sorry.
...

Are you worried about taking a bus in a foreign country? Which bus will you take? How much does it cost? Will you have to change buses? These are all questions that will go through your mind at the bus stop. Don't worry! Bus drivers will help you find your way. Other passengers will too. All you have to do is **ask**!

Useful expressions

Questions to ask at the bus stop
Which bus goes to the airport?
How often does bus number 301 come?
Does the downtown bus stop here?
Where do I catch the bus to the hospital/airport/mall/library/university?
Is this the bus that goes down Main Street?（when you see one coming）

Responses you may hear
I'm sorry, I'm not from here.
The bus comes every fifteen minutes.
The bus comes once an hour.
You need bus #14.
Any bus will take you to the airport.
It will be here any minute.

Talking to the bus driver
Is this an express bus?
How much is the fare to …?
What is the child's fare?
Is there a student fare?
I need to get off at …
Can you tell me when we get to …?
Which is the closest stop to …?
How far is it to …?

Show the courtesy to other passengers
May I sit here?
Would you like my seat?
I'll stand.
I can move over for you.
Excuse me, this is my stop.（If someone is sitting beside you or blocking the door.）

🔊 **5. Listen and repeat. Practice the following conversations with your partner.**

Example 1   Which bus to take
A: I need to get to PCC, but I don't know which bus to catch.
B: Where exactly are you coming from?
A: I'm coming from Fair Oaks and Las Flores Drive in Altadena.
B: Do you have a problem walking a little bit?
A: I don't mind walking.
B: If you walk down Fair Oaks to Altadena Drive, you can catch the 267.
A: Tell me which direction it should be going.
B: Make sure to catch it going west.
A: Where do I get off?
B: You get off on Del Mar and Hill.
A: Thanks for the help.
B: Don't mention it.

Example 2　Where to get off
A: Are you sure that this bus will take us to Santa Anita mall?
B: Yes, it will.
A: You know that for a fact?
B: Yeah, I catch this bus all the time.
A: Is it a very long bus ride?
B: It's about thirty minutes long.
A: Do you know where we get off at?
B: There's a bus stop right behind Macy's.
A: Really, there's a bus stop right by the mall?
B: There's a bus stop in the mall parking lot.
A: That's convenient.
B: Absolutely.

Example 3　Where to change the bus
A: Which bus should I take from PHS to Vons?
B: Can you tell me which Vons you want to go to?
A: I believe that it's on Fair Oaks and Orange Grove.
B: You'll have to catch two different buses to get there.
A: Do you know which buses I need to take?
B: The 268 is the first bus you need to catch.
A: What do I do after I get on the 268?
B: Get off when you get to Fair Oaks and Washington.
A: Then what?
B: Catch the 261 and get off at Vons.
A: That's all?
B: That's all you have to do.

6. Match the words on the left with the correct meanings on the right.

	Terms		Definitions
(1)	**bus fare**	A.	enter the bus
(2)	**bus route**	B.	the way the bus goes; usually associated with a number or place name
(3)	**get off**	C.	the long hall you walk down
(4)	**get on/board**	D.	the amount of money to pay the driver
(5)	**rear seats**	E.	transportation that anyone can use (buses, subways, trains)
(6)	**aisle**	F.	leave the bus
(7)	**courtesy seating**	G.	seating at the back of the bus
(8)	**public transit**	H.	seating for those who need extra time or help to get on or off the bus

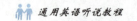

Role-play

Imagine your former classmate comes to visit you from another city. You plan to pay a visit to Turtle-Head Peninsula Park（or Yuantouzhu Park）from your university. However, you don't know the bus route. Create a dialogue to find out how to take the right bus to your destination by asking a passenger who is waiting at the bus station.

🔊 *7. Listen to the dialogue and choose the best answer to the questions below.*

（1） Where is the man going?
  A. To a museum.
  B. To a movie theater.
  C. To a musical comedy.
  D. To a park.

（2） How long will it take the man to get to his destination?
  A. With five minutes.
  B. With ten minutes.
  C. With fifteen minutes.
  D. With twenty minutes.

（3） What time does the place in Question 1 close?
  A. At 4:30 pm.
  B. At 5:00 pm.
  C. At 6:00 pm.
  D. At 6:30 pm.

（4） Where is the man going later downtown?
  A. To a party.
  B. To a restaurant.
  C. To a play.
  D. To a business meeting.

（5） How much will the fare be for the taxi ride, not including a tip?
  A. Between five and ten dollars.
  B. Between ten and fifteen dollars.
  C. Between fifteen and twenty dollars.
  D. More than twenty dollars.

8. Listen to the dialogue again and write in the missing words.

Passenger: Hey Taxi! Ah great. Thanks for (1) _____ over.
Driver: Where to?
Passenger: Well, I'm going to the National Museum of Art, and ...
Driver: Sure. Hop in. No problem. Hang on!
Passenger: Uh. Excuse me, how long does it take to get there?
Driver: Well, that all depends on the (2)_____, but it shouldn't take more than twenty minutes for the average driver. [Oh]. And I'm not average, so we should be able to (3) _____ through traffic and get there in less than twelve minutes.
Passenger: Okay. Uh, sorry for asking [Yeah?], but do you have any idea how much the (4) _____ will be?
Driver: Oh, it shouldn't be more than 18 dollars ... not including a ... uh-hum ... a (5) _____ of course.
Passenger: Oh, and by the way, do you know what time the museum closes?
Driver: Well, I would guess around 6:00 o'clock.
Passenger: Uh, do you have the time?
Driver: Yeah. It's half past four. [Thanks] Uh, this is your first time to the city, right?
Passenger: Yeah. How did you know?
Driver: Well, you can tell (6) _____ from a mile away in this city because they walk down the street looking straight up at the skyscrapers.
Passenger: Was it that obvious?
Driver: Well ...
Passenger: Oh, before I forget, can you recommend any good restaurants downtown that offer meals at a (7) _____ price?
Driver: Umm... Well, the Mexican restaurant, La Fajita, is (8) _____. [Oh] It's not as inexpensive as other places I know, but the (9) _____ is very authentic, [Okay] and the portions are larger than most places I've been to.
Passenger: Sounds great! How do I get there from the museum?
Driver: Well, you can catch the subway right outside the museum. There are buses that run that way, but you would have to (10) _____ a couple of times. And there are taxis too, but they don't run by the museum that often.
Passenger: Okay. Thanks.

Role-play

Practice the conversation with a partner. Then create your own conversation involving a taxi driver and a passenger. Student A will act as a taxi driver. Student B will act as a tourist who lives in downtown and is going to visit Lingshan Buddha. Student A will recommend other tourist attractions and restaurants.

9. **There are quite a few experssions which contain certain words abouttransportation. Use the correct form of the following phrases to fill in the blanks in the sentences below.**

| to sail through | to go overboard | to drive sb mad | to miss the boat |
| to take on board | slow coach | in the same boat | all shipshape |

sail through	to succeed very easily in a test, examination, etc.
go overboard	to react in an immoderate way
drive sb mad	to make sb nervous or worried
miss the boat	to fail to take advantage of an opportunity
take on board	to accept or approve
slow coach	someone who moves slowly
in the same boat	in the same situation or predicament
（all）shipshape	if something is shipshape, it looks tidy, neat, and in good condition

(1) I know someone who is a _____. He never does anything quickly.
(2) Helen _____ all exams when she was at school because she always studied hard.
(3) I think we're all _____ when we try to pronounce English words; they are equally difficult for us.
(4) It _____ when I see people talking on their mobile phones when they are driving their cars! I think it's really dangerous.
(5) We spent ages tidying and cleaning the house so that it was _____ for our grandma.
(6) Last year my English teacher offered us free English lessons but I didn't take the opportunity. Now I want them but she's not offering them any more so I've_____.
(7) He listened carefully to his parents' advice and agreed to act on it. You could say that he _____ all the advice he was given.
(8) Tony has bought a new English dictionary, a dictionary of phrasal verbs and idioms and a subscription to an English newspaper. It's too much. I think he's _____.

2.1.2 Long-distance transportation

🔊 *1. Listen to the dialogue. Write in the missing words.*

Check in at the airport	
Departure time	
Seat preference	
Check-in baggage	
Carry-on baggage	
Boarding/Departure gate No.	

🔊 *2. Listen to the talk and decide whether the following statements are true(T) or false(F).*

(1)	British police uncovered a plan to bomb airports.	T / F
(2)	It is still not 100 percent safe to travel by airplane.	T / F
(3)	Airports have banned liquids from cabin and hand luggage.	T / F
(4)	Mothers have to drink the baby milk to prove it is safe.	T / F
(5)	The new rules have caused very little trouble at airports.	T / F
(6)	Airlines say the measures cannot be continued for a long time.	T / F
(7)	Many business travelers may switch to private jets.	T / F
(8)	Most airlines pay passengers for damage to or loss of personal items.	T / F

🔊 **3. Listen to the talk again and write in the missing words.**

International airports have（1）_____ security controls after British police uncovered a plan to bomb airplanes crossing the Atlantic. Five years after the 911 attacks, terrorists are still trying（2）_____ to get past airport safety checks. Last week's failed bombings of transatlantic planes are（3）_____ air travel is still not 100 percent safe. A gang planned to make bombs on board airliners using liquids, which X-ray machines cannot detect. Airports have now banned（4）_____ from carry-on luggage. For many destinations, only essential items can be checked in. Everything else must（5）_____ in the airplane's cargo area. This includes laptop computers and even electronic car keys. Mothers have to drink the baby milk they carry（6）_____ is not dangerous.

The new measures are causing a（7）_____ at major airports. London's Heathrow has cancelled one（8）_____ daily flights. Airlines are angry at the cancellations. They think the new security controls cannot work（9）_____ period of time. Travelling has also become more difficult for passengers. Business travelers may switch to private jets（10）_____ carry their computers onto the airplane. Many executives may consider the small extra cost would be better than having no hand baggage. Economy class passengers are（11）_____ about their valuables, which might get lost, stolen or broken after check-in. Most airlines do not pay passengers for damage（12）_____ personal items.

🔊 **4. Listen to the flight safety instructions carefully and match the verbs or phrases on the left with the appropriate expressions on the right.**

	Verbs/Phrases		Nouns
(1)	stow	A.	smoke detectors
(2)	turn off	B.	the exit nearest you
(3)	find	C.	your carry-on baggage
(4)	place ... over your nose and mouth	D.	your oxygen mask
(5)	fasten	E.	smoking
(6)	(be) not allowed	F.	mobile phones and other electronic devices
(7)	tamper with, disable, destroy	G.	your seat belt

5. Listen again. Fill in the dos box with what you should do based on the safety instructions and fill in the don'ts box with what you shouldn't do. Then discuss with your partner to share what you have written down.

Dos

_____
_____
_____
_____
_____

Don'ts

_____
_____
_____
_____
_____
_____

2.2 Critical thinking and speaking

Task 1

Internet transforms the way people hail a taxi

The Internet is a game changer that's transformed the retail industry, the gaming industry and now it's set to turn another industry upside down: the taxi industry. Here are a few Chinese taxi-booking apps, some of which are the survivors in the competition while others are just passers-by.

Yaoyao Taxi

Developed by Beijing Juhezhongxin Information Technology Co. Ltd, Yaoyao Taxi relies on its comprehensive rating and guarantee system to avoid breaching appointment. It has also formed a strategic partnership with official government taxi-hailing service 96106.

Kuaidi Taxi

Developed by Hangzhou Kuaizhi Technology Co. Ltd, the app's name literally means fast taxi hailing. It is not only one of the first taxi-hailing apps on smartphones but also the first taxi app to support payment by Alipay, the online payment platform developed by Alibaba Group. In December 2013, Kuaidi Taxi covered more than 40 cities, securing one of the top ranks in the industry.

Module 2　Transportation

Didi Taxi

Didi Taxi, which was developed by Beijing Orange Technology Co. Ltd and launched on September 9, 2012, is already being used by more than 3,000 taxi drivers to find customers in Beijing alone. At its primary market Beijing, the app has 85 percent answering rate, with 90 percent at off-peak hours.

WeChat

Internet giant Tencent also joined the club, adding taxi-hailing function to its popular online messaging app WeChat. It has a user base of 400 million.

1. *Read the passage and fill in the following table.*

Battle between taxi app Didi and Kuaidi

The two Chinese taxi-booking apps for smartphones have been heating up their battle backed by Internet giants Tencent and Alipay.

Didi, indicating the beep of a car, is working with Tencent's WeChat, while Kuaidi, meaning to find a taxi swiftly, has joined hands with Alipay as the payment method.

They are now both applying financial means to attract users and drivers: They will give promotion fees to taxi drivers for each deal made, and also save 10 *yuan* for each taxi passenger when a customer takes a taxi through the app and pays the fare through the mobile payment method.

Didi requires the customers to connect their bank cards with WeChat account and then 10 *yuan* will be deducted directly from the fare, and the taxi drivers will get another 10 *yuan*. WeChat is a mobile comprehensive service platform by Internet giant Tencent offering communication, shopping, payment, game, etc.

Kuaidi needs the users' Alipay account and will return 10 *yuan* back to the payment account, and the money will be available in 3 days for withdraw or consumptions, and the drivers will receive 15 *yuan*. Alipay is a mobile payments platform rolled out by e-commerce giant Alibaba.

Didi received $18 million from GSR Ventures and Tencent in the previous two financing rounds. In the third financing round, it received $100 million, $60 million from CITIC Private Equity Funds Management Co., and $30 million from Tencent.

Kuaidi in June 2013, received $8 million from Alibaba, and merged another taxi service company Bumblebee.

	Didi	Kuaidi
Amount of users	30 million	23 million
Orders per day	500,000	300,000

Culture notes **How to use a taxi app**

1. Download it from app store.
2. Open it and input the destination and click "calling".
3. Wait for the taxi. When the order is accepted, some information will be showed including drivers' name, drivers' company, car number, and waiting time.
4. Input charge fee showed in taximeter, and click "payment" when you arrive.

	Didi	Kuaidi
Cooperation partner		
Requirements for using		
Incentive to users		
Incentive to drivers		

Module 2　Transportation

Pair work

2. Each of you will represent one company in the following chart. Tell your partner the policy change of your company according to the chronological order.

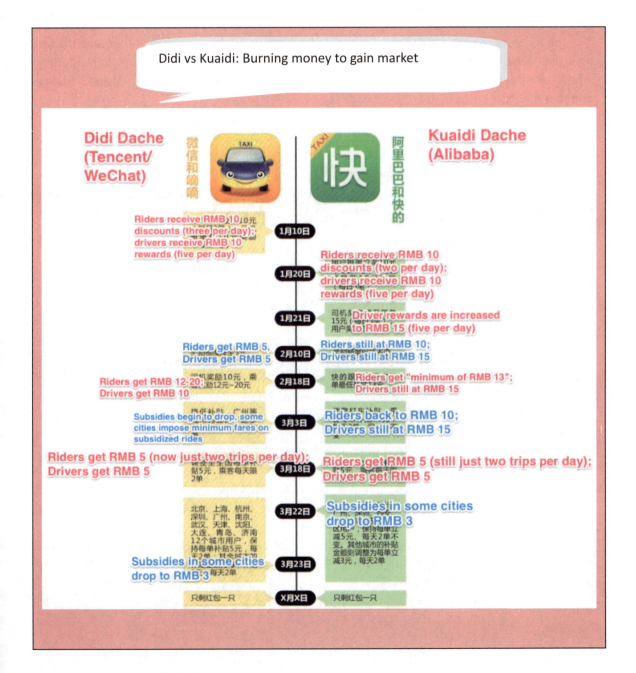

Task 2 *Read the passage and check true or false. Then work in pairs and compare your answers.*

Car-booking apps start moving up the ladder

The battle of the taxi hailing apps seems to have slowed, with market leaders Kuaidi Dache and Didi Dache calling an end in early August to their month-long marketing campaigns, during which both poured hundreds of millions of yuan into subsidies and cash rebates for taxi drivers and passengers.

But a new competition targeting wealthy travelers is now picking up speed, as Kuaidi, which is backed by e-commerce giant Alibaba Group Holding Ltd, launched a new car-booking brand called Kuaidi One that offers pickup services with luxury cars and chauffeur services.

Didi, which is supported by Alibaba's rival Tencent Holdings Ltd, is reportedly set to launch a similar service in late August. It is said to be holding training sessions for drivers so they can offer better services to high-end customers. The company, however, denied such reports when reached by *China Daily*.

Along with the two major players in ride-summoning apps, Beijing-based Baidu Inc teamed up earlier this month with car rental company Yongche to launch a car-booking service called Baidu Zhuanche, a high-end pickup service for business travelers.

With Baidu jumping in, the sector is now a battlefield for all three of China's Internet giants.

Rather than sending regular taxis to pick customers up, these apps offer a wide array of luxury automobiles to choose from, well-trained drivers and such in-car facilities as bottled water, umbrellas, WiFi and even slippers.

Neither Baidu nor Yongche would reveal financial details of their partnership, but Yongche said in a statement on Aug. 4 that by teaming up with Baidu, it will give its mobile users access to Baidu's mapping app.

Yongche, founded in 2010, is the largest Internet-based car-sharing service company in China, involving more than 50,000 vehicles in 74 cities.

Its team-up with Baidu is expected to challenge not only Kuaidi and Didi but also its Western counterpart Uber, a US ride-summoning mobile app that entered Chinese market in February.

Statistics from Analysys International, a Beijing-based Internet consultancy, showed that the online car rental market in China climbed 22.5 percent quarter-on-quarter to 3.98 billion yuan（$484 million）in the quarter ending in June.

Booking luxury cars with chauffeurs through an app is a niche market still in its infancy in China, but it shows great potential for future growth, said Li Zumin, manager of Kuaidi One.

"The difference between traveling in a taxi and a high-end car with a chauffeur is like the difference between staying in a regular inn and a five-star hotel. Even though the luxury hotel is more expensive, there are still people who want to pay more to enjoy better services, environment and facilities," said Li.

Li said through cooperating with car rental companies, Kuaidi One manages a fleet of more than 1 million cars across China, ranging from Volkswagen, Mercedes-Benz and Bentley.

The trial operation of Kuaidi One over the past several months has received positive feedback from the market, with monthly revenue exceeding 10 million *yuan*, according to the company.

Zhu Zhengyu, an analyst with Analysys International, said the market for high-end car-bookings is not so big as the taxi-hailing one, but the profit margin is higher.

In big cities such as Beijing, it is difficult to own a car because of restrictions on issuing new license plates, he said.

Moreover, with the government's ongoing campaign to cut down on the official cars, these high-end service providers are expected to see an increasing number of orders from corporate clients, Zhu said.

The latest policy guidelines mean that most government cars—about 90 percent of the total number—will be auctioned off, and only those for minister-level officials and for public security purposes, such as police cars, will be kept.

Officials will be getting monthly commuting allowances ranging from 500 *yuan* to 1,300 *yuan*.

Wang Xiaofeng, an analyst at Forrester Research, said it makes sense for both Alibaba-backed Kuaidi and Tencent-backed Didi to enter the high-end car-hailing market as the two companies have invested heavily to build up their brands.

Statistics from Analysys International show that by the end of June, the number of accounts registered with taxi-hailing apps totaled 130 million, with Kuaidi accounting for 53.57 percent and Didi for 45.56 percent.

Wang said that ride-summoning apps are a strategic sector for Baidu, Alibaba and Tencent to carry out their location-based services.

"The apps help gather a lot of data about the consumption habits of users, such as where they usually go on a Thursday night. The information can be useful for these Internet giants to offer other services, such as coupons or cinema tickets," she said, adding the data concerning high-end well-spending users can be even more valuable.

	True	False
◆ Kuaidi started a new car-booking brand called Kuaidi One.	☐	☐
◆ Didi supported by Alibaba Group is set to launch a similar service.	☐	☐
◆ Baidu Inc. launched a car-booking service called Baidu Zhuanche alone.	☐	☐
◆ Those high-end apps offer luxury cars and chauffeur services.	☐	☐
◆ A foreign-funded ride-summoning app has entered Chinese market.	☐	☐
◆ Hailing luxury cars through an app is not a growth market in China.	☐	☐
◆ The trial operation of Kuaidi One for months has been unsuccessful.	☐	☐
◆ High-end car-booking apps have a higher profit margin.	☐	☐
◆ Both Didi and Kuaidi invested heavily in brand-building.	☐	☐
◆ The apps help collect data about the consumption habits of users.	☐	☐

Assignment

Read the passage again and discuss the following questions with your partner:

（1）Do you have any experience of using a car-booking app? If yes, share your feelings. If not, are you willing to try?

（2）Work out a list of "Pros and Cons" of car-booking apps. If you are asked to offer some suggestion to improve their service, what will you say?

Module 2 Transportation

Self-assessment

Review the content covered in this module. How well can you do each of the following?

	very well	well	not well
I know how to talk about using different means of transportation.	○	○	○
I know how to behave properly in public or private transportation.	○	○	○
I know how to choose the appropriate transportation to get to my destination.	○	○	○
I know how to book a taxi through a mobile phone app.	○	○	○

Module 3
Telecommunications

While marveling at the constant and dazzling innovation of information technologies,
- do you have any general ideas about the development of telecommunications?
- can you make phone calls in an appropriate and polite manner?
- how far away are you from Internet addiction?
- can you protect yourself against cybercrimes?

3.1 Listening and speaking

3.1.1 Development of telecommunications

1. Complete the statements on the next page with proper means of telecommunications illustrated in the pictures.

radio

television

mobile phone

carrier pigeon

landline

flag semaphore

telegraph

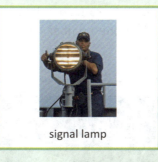
signal lamp

fax

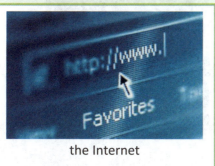
the Internet

beacons or relay fires

(1) _____ were fires lit at well-known locations on hills or high places, used either as lighthouses for navigation at sea, or for signaling over land that enemy troops were approaching, in order to alert defenses.

(2) _____ is a visual system for sending information by means of two flags that are held one in each hand, using an alphabetic code based on the position of the signaler's arms.

(3) A _____ is a visual signaling device for optical communication (typically using Morse code).

(4) _____ is a system of sending sound over a distance by transmitting electrical signals.

(5) _____ is the long distance transmission of textual/symbolic messages without the physical exchange of an object bearing the message.

(6) A _____ refers to a phone that uses a metal wire telephone line for transmission.

(7) A _____, also known as a cellular phone, cell phone, or hand phone, is a phone that can make and receive telephone calls over a radio link while moving around a wide geographic area.

(8) _____ is a telecommunication medium that is used for transmitting and receiving moving images and sound.

(9) The _____ is a global system of interconnected computer networks that use the standard Internet protocol suite (TCP/IP) to link several billion devices worldwide.

(10) A _____ or messenger pigeon is a homing pigeon that is used to carry messages.

(11) _____ (short for facsimile), sometimes called telecopying or telefax, is the telephonic transmission of scanned printed material (both text and images), normally to a telephone number connected to a printer or other output device.

Module 3 Telecommunications

🔊 *2. Listen to the short passage about the development of telecommunications. While listening, please note down the missing information. You will hear the passage twice.*

> **Word tips**
>
> **optimize** /ˈɒptɪmaɪz/   **instantaneously** /ˌɪnstənˈteɪnɪəslɪ/
>
> ✓ To **optimize** a plan, system, or machine means to arrange or design it so that it operates as smoothly and efficiently as possible.
> ✓ Something that is **instantaneous** happens immediately and very quickly.

Telecommunications, or telecom, is the transmission of (1) _____ over long distances. It began with the invention of the (2) _____ in 1837, followed by the (3) _____ in 1876. (4) _____ broadcasts began in the late 1800s and the first (5) _____ broadcasts started in the early 1900s. Today, popular forms of telecommunications include the (6) _____ and (7) _____ networks.

Early telecommunications (8) _____ used analog signals, which were (9) _____ over copper wires. Today, telephone and cable companies still use these same lines, though most transmissions are now (10) _____. For this reason, most new telecommunications wiring is done with cables that are (11) _____ for digital communication, such as fiber-optic cables and digital phone lines.

Since both analog and digital communications are based on (12) _____ signals, transmitted data is received almost (13) _____, regardless of the distance. This allows people to (14) _____ across the street or across the globe. So whether you're watching TV, sending an email to a co-worker, or (15) _____, you can thank telecommunications for making it possible.

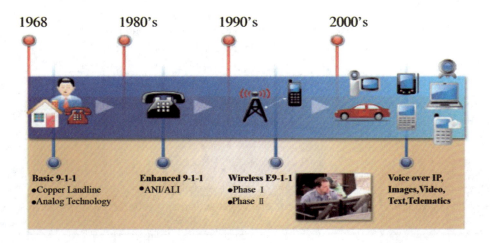

3.1.2 Telephone skills

1. Choose an appropriate word from the given choices according to the context.

（1）A telephone _____ or provider is a company that provides telephone services both local and long-distance to customers.

A. install
B. message
C. carrier
D. call

（2）In the US, there is a lot of _____ in the telecommunication field now so telephone service prices have come down in the past twenty years. Many companies are trying hard to get and keep customers.

A. message
B. competition
C. number
D. page

（3）We pay a monthly service fee and, in our plan, we are able to make an _____ amount of local calls per month. That means that we can call anyone and talk for as long as we want so long as they live in the specified vicinity.

A. limited
B. unlimited
C. long-distance
D. installed

（4）I just moved and I have to get my phone _____-up soon. Luckily, I have my cell phone but the rates are really pricey during the day.

A. deregulated
B. answered
C. called
D. hooked

（5）I need to get a _____ carrier soon. I want to call my parents on a regular basis and I can't call them with my regular, local package because they're on the west coast and we're on the east coast.

A. long-distance
B. message
C. local
D. voicemail

（6）I'm going to get _____ soon so that people can leave me messages on my landline if I'm not home. I hate not knowing who called and, this way, I'll be able to respond to calls left by anyone who chooses to leave me a message.

A. cordless
B. voicemail
C. cable
D. fees

（7）I'm also going to get call-_____ thrown into my phone package. That way, if I'm on the phone with someone, I'll hear a sound and know that someone else is trying to reach me. All you have to do is press one button to put the first caller on hold in order to answer the second caller who is trying to get through. Modern conveniences are great.

A. mobile
B. waiting
C. local
D. hook-up

（8）I want to buy a _____ phone so that I can walk around my house and talk on the phone at the same time. I don't like being confined to my desk and the telephone cord is so short.

A. monopoly
B. collect
C. package
D. cordless

（9）I'm in the process of hooking-up my phone service. The telephone company is sending a technician out today to _____ my landline. I can't wait to have a phone again!

A. fee
B. cable
C. install
D. hang-up

（10）Why didn't you _____ me a message? I didn't even know that you called. Please do that the next time you call so that I don't miss any urgent matters.

A. leave
B. miss
C. turn
D. call

40

Module 3 Telecommunications

2. Talking on the phone might be challenging without face-to-face interaction. Luckily some expressions and skills may help you make it easier. You will hear two telephone conversations. Please put a tick (√) for the steps covered in each conversation. Then listen again and fill in the blanks.

Steps	Conversation 1	Conversation 2
Answering the phone	√	√
Introducing the caller/ phone maker		
Asking to speak with someone		
Taking a message for someone		
Confirming information		
Finishing a conversation		

Conversation 1

Leslie:	Hello?
Cameron:	Hi, (1) _____ Leslie?
Leslie:	Yes. (2) _____?
Cameron:	It's Cameron here. Is Maria (3) _____?
Leslie:	No, she just (4) _____ out for a moment. Can I take a message?
Cameron:	Yes, thanks. (5) _____ ask her to meet me at the Capitol 4 movie theatre at 7 pm tonight?
Leslie:	Sure. Just let me write that down. Oh Cameron, could you hold on (6) _____? I have to take another call.
Cameron:	No problem.
Leslie:	Hi. Sorry about that. Now could you please (7) _____ that information? I didn't have a pen handy.
Cameron:	Sure. It's the Capitol 4 theatre at 7 o'clock.
Leslie:	Okay, I've (8) _____ it. Is there anything else?
Cameron:	No, that's great.
Leslie:	Okay. Uh-oh, there's my other line again. I'd better (9) _____.
Cameron:	Okay, thanks again. Bye for now.
Leslie:	(10) _____.

41

Conversation 2

Receptionist:	Thank you for phoning Maple Dental Clinic. Sylvia（1）_____. How can I help you?
Thelma:	Hi, Sylvia. （2）_____ Thelma Woods calling. How are you today?
Receptionist:	I'm fine, Mrs. Woods. How are you?
Thelma:	Well, actually, I have a bit of a sore tooth. I was hoping Dr. Morris would have some time to see me this week.
Receptionist:	I'm （3）_____ he's booked this week. I can put you in for 2 pm next Tuesday. How does that sound?
Thelma:	That would be great.
Receptionist:	I'll have to give you the address of our new office.
Thelma:	Oh, that's right, you moved.
Receptionist:	Yes, we moved downtown. Do you have（4）_____?
Thelma:	Could you （5）_____ a moment please? ... Okay, go ahead, Sylvia.
Receptionist:	Okay, we are at 723 Baltic Avenue. Suite 004.
Thelma:	（6）_____ spelling that for me?
Receptionist:	Sure. That's seven-twenty-three Baltic—B（7）_____ Bravo, A as in Alpha, L as in Lima, T as in tango, I as in India, and C as in Charlie. And it's suite zero zero four.
Thelma:	Okay, great. I'll see you on Tuesday then.
Receptionist:	Okay. （8）_____ calling. See you then.
Thelma:	Thanks. Bye.

Module 3 Telecommunications

🔊 **3. Now you are going to hear two telephone dialogues. While listening, please take down the messages for the speakers who are answering the phone.**

Dialogue 1

To: _____

Caller: _____

Message:
_____
_____
_____
_____
_____

Dialogue 2

To: _____

Caller: _____

Message:
_____
_____
_____
_____
_____
_____

Role-play

4. Work in pairs and role-play the telephone dialogues according to the given situations on Page 44. You may refer to useful expressions on Page 45 to make calls.

43

Situations

	A	B
(1)	You are calling your friend Ken. You want to invite him to a party this Friday.	You answer the phone. The person on the other end of the line wants to speak to Ken. You don't know anyone named Ken.
(2)	You promised your mother that you would water her plants while she was away on vacation. You forgot. The plants are dead. The phone rings.	You are away on vacation in San Francisco. You have a lot of beautiful plants. Call your son/daughter to find out how your plants are doing.
(3)	You have not finished writing your English essay. Call your teacher and ask if you can turn it in late.	You are an English teacher. The phone rings. It's one of your students.
(4)	You need to telephone your partner at his or her office. You planned to be home early today so you could go out for dinner together but you have to stay at work until very late. Telephone your partner's office and tell him/her the bad news. Make sure you say sorry.	You work at Smith and Jones Publishing Limited, in an office with one other person. He or she is in an important meeting and you are taking messages if anyone telephones. Answer the telephone and take a message.
(5)	You met someone new in your class. You want to invite your new friend out for a coffee on Saturday. Telephone your friend and make a date.	You met someone in your class but you didn't really like them very much and you don't want to be with them outside the class. Answer the telephone. Try to be polite but say "no".

Useful expressions

Telephone language

Answering the phone	Hello?（informal） Thank you for calling Boyz Autobody. Jody speaking. How can I help you? Doctor's office.
Introducing yourself	Hey George. It's Lisa calling. （informal） Hello, this is Julie Madison calling. Hi, it's Gerry from the dentist's office here. This is she.* / Speaking.* *The person answering says this if the caller does not recognize their voice.
Asking to speak with someone	Is Fred in?（informal） Is Jackson there, please?（informal） Can I talk to your sister?（informal） May I speak with Mr. Green, please? Would the doctor be in/available?
Connecting someone	Just a second. /Hang on one second. I'll get him.（informal） Please hold and I'll put you through to his office. One moment please.
Making special requests	Could you please repeat that? Would you mind spelling that for me? Could you speak up a little please? Can you speak a little slower please? My English isn't very strong. Can you call me back? I think we have a bad connection. Can you please hold for a minute? I have another call.
Taking a message for someone	Sammy's not in. Who's this?（informal） I'm sorry, Lisa's not here at the moment. Can I ask who's calling? I'm afraid he's stepped out. Would you like to leave a message? He's on lunch right now. Who's calling please? I'll let him know you called. I'll make sure she gets the message.
Leaving a message with someone	Yes. Can you tell him his wife called, please? No, that's okay. I'll call back later. Thanks. Could you ask him to call Brian when he gets in? Thanks. My number is 222-3456, extension 12.
Confirming information	Okay, I've got it all down. Let me repeat that just to make sure. Did you say 555 Charles Street? You said your name was John, right?
Finishing a conversation	Well, I guess I better get going. Talk to you soon. Thanks for calling. Bye for now. I have to let you go now. I have another call coming through. I better run. I'm afraid that's my other line. I'll talk to you again soon. Bye.

3.1.3 Internet addiction

1. Match the following synonyms.

（1）addiction　　　　A. different
（2）forgetful　　　　B. expect
（3）various　　　　　C. impacting
（4）resembling　　　D. immersed
（5）affecting　　　　E. obsession
（6）quizzed　　　　　F. communication
（7）absorbed　　　　G. looking like
（8）anticipate　　　H. absent-minded
（9）interaction　　　I. moan
（10）complain　　　　J. questioned

2. Listen to the passage related to Internet addiction and fill in the missing information.

Internet addiction	A problem that many of us have but are not （1）_____ of.
	Millions of us are （2）_____ to being online.
Impacts of the Internet on our life	This is a growing problem that is making us more （3）_____.
	Technology is （4）_____ people.
	More and more, life is resembling （5）_____.
	We are living in （6） "_____" which is negatively affecting our real-life relationships.
Seven indicators of "tech overload"	Ten percent of young people had what she called "（7）_____".
	• You （8）_____ before doing other things.
	• You always anticipate and look forward to your next （9）_____.
	• You say "（10）_____" when someone wants you.
	• Your interaction with others also says a lot about how important the Internet is compared with （11）_____.
	• You lie about （12）_____ or choose to （13）_____ instead of going out with others.
	• The "online lift" stops you being （14）_____.
	• Others complain about （15）_____.

Module 3   Telecommunications

3. **Now you will hear the news report on "Young Net Addicts on the Rise". Listen and choose the best answer for each question.**

(1) How many young people are said to be addicted to the Internet in 2009?
   A. Almost half the figure for 2005.
   B. 24 million.
   C. One in seven Internet users.

(2) What measures did the government take to fight Internet addiction among young people?
   A. Setting up rehabilitation schools, camps and clinics.
   B. Closing down cyber cafes.
   C. Installing filtering software.

(3) What was China's young Internet population (netizens younger than 19) in 2009?
   A. 384 million.
   B. About 120 million.
   C. 30 percent of the national Internet population.

(4) What percentage of Internet users aged 18 to 23 are said to be addicted?
   A. 15.6 percent of netizens.
   B. 8.8 percent of Internet users.
   C. 30 percent of netizens.

(5) How was the result of the years of efforts by the authorities to try and prevent children from getting addicted?
   A. Ineffective.
   B. Hard to tell.
   C. Effective.

Group discussion

4. Suppose one of your classmates is so indulged in playing PC games and often skips classes. Could you offer some suggestions to help him out? You may use the tips given below to expand your ideas.

Tips for dealing with computer addiction
- Write down the activities you miss out and decrease your Internet time to pursue some of them.
- Set reasonable Internet use goals and stick to them.
- Alter your routine to break your usage patterns.
- Seek out friends and acquaintances.
- Stay connected to the offline world.
- Treat the Internet as a tool.
- ...

3.1.4 Information security

🔊 1. Now you are going to hear a passage about protecting personal information on mobile devices. Listen to the first part and find out the missing information in the table below.

Mobile devices	include (1) _____, (2) _____, tablets and USB keys
Advantages	• offer tremendous (3) _____
	• increasingly (4) _____ and can hold (5) _____ amounts of personal data
Disadvantages	• also raise important new risks for (6) _____ and the protection of (7) _____
	• small but easy to (8) _____
	• also vulnerable to threats such as (9) _____
	• Once your personal information is compromised, it could cause you significant personal and (10) _____ harm.

🔊 2. Listen to the second part and complete the following ten tips.

10 tips for protecting privacy

(1) _____ yourself about your mobile devices and how to enable or add privacy and security tools.

(2) _____ the personal information that is stored on mobile devices to that which is absolutely necessary.

(3) Ensure that mobile devices are protected with _____ passwords. Never rely on factory setting passwords.

(4) Use an _____ feature so that a password is required to access information on mobile devices.

(5) Consider using an _____ encryption technology to provide added protection for personal information on mobile devices.

(6) _____ anti-virus, anti-spyware and firewall programs on your mobile device and keep those programs up-to-date.

(7) Don't send personal data over _____ networks—at cafes, for example—unless you have added security such as a Virtual Private Network (VPN).

(8) Never leave your mobile device _____ in a public place or a vehicle.

(9) Ensure that data stored on mobile devices that are no longer needed is purged prior to _____.

(10) Check the _____ for your mobile device for further information.

3.2 Critical thinking and speaking

Task 1

Social networking services in America

Read the following paragraphs about social networking services in America. Choose appropriate words or expressions on the right for the incomplete statements.

47% of American adults used social networking sites like Facebook, MySpace, Twitter, LinkedIn, and Classmates.com in 2011, up from 26% in 2008. On social media sites like these, users may (1) _____ biographical profiles, (2) _____ with friends and strangers, (3) _____ research, and (4) _____ thoughts, photos, music, links, and more.	A. communicate B. develop C. do D. share
Proponents of social networking sites say that the online communities promote (5) _____ with friends and family; offer teachers, librarians, and students valuable (6) _____; facilitate (7) _____; and (8) disseminate _____ rapidly.	A. access to educational support and materials B. increased interaction C. social and political
Opponents of social networking say that the sites (9) _____ face-to-face communication; (10) _____ time on frivolous activity; (11) _____ children's brains and behavior making them more prone to ADHD; (12) _____ users to predators like pedophiles and burglars; and (13) _____ false and potentially dangerous information.	A. alter B. expose C. prevent D. spread E. waste

Task 2

Social networking services (SNS)

Discussions

- Have you ever signed on any social networking services? If yes, what site or software are you using?
- What are the typical features or functions of social networking services?
- What type of information do you put on social networking sites?
- How long do you stay on your SNS every day? Or how often do you check the updates on your SNS?
- Are you addicted to SNS? Or can you live without SNS?

Task 3

Social networking sites: Friend or foe?

Debate

(1) Work in groups to brainstorm supportive arguments for the five pairs of statements.
(2) The teacher divides the class into two sides.
(3) Follow the format of a 10-minute debate on Page 52.

Pros	Cons
(1) Social networking sites spread information faster than any other media.	(1) Social media enables the spread of unreliable and false information.
(2) Social networking sites help students do better at school.	(2) Students who are heavy social media users tend to have lower grades.
(3) Social networking sites allow people to improve their relationships and make new friends.	(3) Social networking sites can lead to stress and offline relationship problems.
(4) Being a part of a social networking site can increase a person's quality of life and reduce the risk of health problems.	(4) The use of social networking sites is correlated with personality and brain disorders, such as self-centered personalities and addictive behaviors.
(5) Corporations and small businesses use social media to benefit themselves and consumers.	(5) Social networking sites' advertising practices may constitute an invasion of privacy.

Tips

The format of a 10-minute debate

- A coin toss will decide the choice of sides, followed by a five-minute preparation period before the debate begins. Remember, you need to consider arguments and critiques for both sides of the proposal, even though you are arguing for only one side.
- First Affirmative Speech is to be no longer than one minute in length.
- Questioning by Negative Team will last for one minute.
- First Negative Speech is to be no longer than one minute in length.
- Questioning by Affirmative Team will last for one minute.
- Three minutes to prepare final argument: Rebuttal Speech.
- One minute for Negative Rebuttal Speech.
- One minute for Affirmative Rebuttal Speech.
  （note: in the Rebuttal, the speaker may not introduce new material that has not already been mentioned in the debate.）
- Critique of debate and decision of judges.

Cybercrimes

Read the following article about cybercrimes and choose an appropriate subheading for each paragraph.

A. Identify theft
B. Storing illegal information
C. Computer viruses
D. Fraud
E. Illegal gambling

Cybercrimes are criminal acts that use the computer or the Internet. These types of crimes are prevalent in modern technological society and are becoming more high profile as a greater number of serious crimes are committed. The US Department of Justice recognizes three types of cybercrimes: those that use the computer as a weapon; those that use the computer as an accessory to a crime; or those that make the computer a target of a crime. Most crimes are traditional in nature and use a computer or the Internet to break the law.

1. _____.
Some criminals use the Internet to break into victims' online financial accounts, taking passwords, money and sensitive information. Others create online centers for trafficking stolen identity information. With more and more people conducting business online and using the Internet to pay bills, the number of identity theft victims has risen. People that use birthdays, their children's names and pet's names as passwords are typically more at risk for identity theft.

2. _____.
Criminals and pedophiles often use the Internet to obtain and transfer illegal images, such as child pornography. Even storing or saving these types of images on a computer is illegal. Other criminals use their computer databases to store illegal information, including confidential intellectual property.

3. _____.
Computer hackers are digital age criminals that can bring down large infrastructures with a single keystroke emitting a computer virus. These types of viruses are macro or binary. Macro viruses attack a specific program, while binary viruses attack data or attach to program files. Hacking into a business' intranet and uploading viruses to the code are examples of these types of crimes. Private citizens are targets of computer viruses when visiting websites with encrypted viruses or opening emails infected with viruses. One of the most famous computer viruses is the Trojan virus.

4. _____.
In the digital age, many criminals easily commit fraud against unsuspecting victims by misrepresenting the facts. For example, an employee intentionally inputs false information into the company database or intranet. Or consider the "Nigerian prince email", where an online predator

attempts to steal money from targeted consumers by gaining access to a shared bank account.

5. _____.

  Gambling is illegal in many US states, and is prohibited online unless you are physically located in a state that allows it. However, the 2008 Internet Skill Game Licensing and Control Act was introduced to Congress and states that players may participate in skill games, such as mah jong and poker, but not in pure luck games. If the player is under the age of 21, he cannot legally gamble in any state. Games that involve monetary transactions, such as transfers to and from credit cards and bank accounts, are considered illegal, so gamblers cannot legally collect their winnings.

****

Assignment

Research: How to protect yourself from cyber crimes

Directions:
1. Visit websites to collect ways of protecting yourself against cybercrimes.
2. Prepare a 5-minute-long presentation to share your findings with the whole class.

Self-assessment

Review the content covered in this module. How well can you do each of the following?

	very well	well	not well
I know about means of telecommunications.	○	○	○
I know how to make phone calls.	○	○	○
I know how to fight againt computer addiction.	○	○	○
I know how to protect myself from cybercrimes.	○	○	○

Module 4 Review

| Note-taking skills | Further listening and speaking | Communication bank |

4.1 Note-taking skills

4.1.1 The Cornell Method

The Cornell Method provides a systematic format for condensing and organizing notes without laborious recopying. After writing the notes in the main space, use the left-hand space to label each idea and detail with a key word or "cue".

Divide the paper into three sections.

- Draw a dark horizontal line about 5 or 6 lines from the bottom. Use a heavy magic marker to draw the line so that it is clear.
- Draw a dark vertical line about 2 inches from the left side of the paper from the top to the horizontal line.

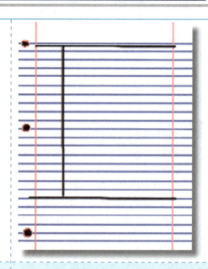

Document

- Write the course name, date, and topic at the top of each page.

Write notes.

- The large box to the right is for writing notes.

- Skip a line between ideas and topics.

- Don't use complete sentences. Use abbreviations whenever possible. Develop shorthand of your own, such as "&" for the word "and".

Review and clarify.

- Review the notes as soon as possible after class.
- Pull out main ideas, key points, dates, and people, and write these in the left column.

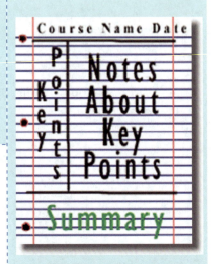

Summarize.

- Write a summary of main ideas in the bottom section.

Study your notes.

- Re-read your notes in the right column.
- Spend most of your time studying the ideas in the left column and the summary at the bottom. These are the most important ideas and will probably include most of the information that you will be tested on.

The outlining method

Dash or indented outlining is usually best except for some science classes such as physics or math.

(1) The information which is most general begins at the left with each more specific group of facts indented with spaces to the right.

(2) The relationships between the different parts are carried out through indenting.

(3) No numbers, letters, or Roman numerals are needed.

Example

- Extrasensory perceptions
    - Definition: means of perceiving without use of sense organs.
        - three kinds
            - telepathy: sending messages
            - clairvoyance: forecasting the future
            - psychokinesis: perceiving events external to situation
        - current status
            - no current research to support or refute
            - few psychologists say impossible
            - door open to future

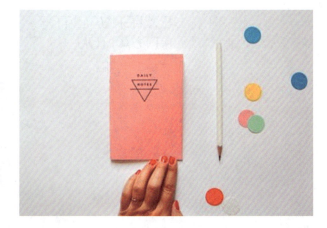

The mapping method

Mapping is a method that uses comprehension/concentration skills and evolves in a note-taking form which relates each fact or idea to every other fact or idea. Mapping is a graphic representation of the content of a lecture. It is a method that maximizes active participation, affords immediate knowledge as to its understanding, and emphasizes critical thinking.

When to use

Use the method when the lecture content is heavy and well-organized. It may also be used effectively when you have a guest lecturer and have no idea how the lecture is going to be presented.

Example:

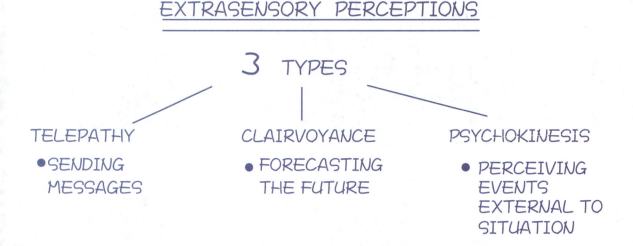

Signal words in talk

Signal supporting material

"On the other hand …"

"On the contrary …"

"For example …"

"Similarly …"

"In contrast …"

"Also …"

"Further …"

"Furthermore …"

"As an example …"

"For instance …"

Common signals

"There are three reasons why …"
   (HERE THEY COME!)

"First … Second … Third …" （THERE THEY ARE!）

"And most important …" （A MAIN IDEA!）

"A major development …" （A MAIN IDEA AGAIN!）

Conclusion or summary

- "Therefore …"

- "In conclusion …"

- "As a result …"

- "Finally …"

- "In summary …"

- "From this we see …"

Signal importance

"Now this is important …"

"Remember that …"

"The important idea is that …"

"The basic concept here is …"

4.1.2 Note-taking practice

> **Culture notes**
> Culture shock is very natural occurrence when traveling to a new culture. Keeping an open mind and being flexible will help you adjust.

I. Pre-listening exercises

What is culture shock and what are the stages of this event?

II. Listening exercises

🔊 1. Listen to the talk and take notes while listening. Choose one type of note-taking skills mentioned previously.

_____
_____
_____
_____
_____
_____

🔊 2. Listen to the talk again. Then fill in the blanks according to what you hear.

Culture shock

Well, I think (1) _____ speaking, we could say that there are four stages to culture shock. First of all, the "(2) _____" stage. Uh, to the visitor, everything seems new, quaint, and (3) _____. The food, the surroundings, the buildings. And it produces a feeling of euphoria, and a desire to look around, to experiment, to (4) _____.

The next stage is the "horror" stage, where the (5) _____ wears off, and the visitor sees the country from a different (6) _____, and often begins to criticize the country, the life, and the (7) _____ of the people.

The next stage, we could say, is the "humor" stage, where people begin to (8) _____ back and laugh at their (9) _____ in the earlier stages.

And the final stage, we could say, is the "home" stage where people begin to feel at home, enjoy (10) _____ in that foreign country.

4.2 Further listening and speaking

4.2.1 Taped library tour

Helpful tips

More and more websites contain online books, magazines, and newspapers to assist in your research, and this is particularly helpful when you live in an area without easy access to a library.

I. Pre-listening exercises

Write down as many different types of resources and services you can find at a library (e.g., magazines, copy service, etc.). If you had to write a research paper on African lions, what steps would you take to find information in the library (without using the Internet)?

II. Listening exercises

1. **Listen to the talk and answer the questions by making choices.**

   (1) Where would you go to check out books?
   A. On Level 1.　　B. On Level 2.
   C. On Level 3.　　D. On Level 4.

   (2) Where is the most likely place to find a book on learning to speak French?
   A. On Level 1.　　B. On Level 2.
   C. On Level 3.　　D. On Level 4.

   (3) Where would you find a January 1996 issue of *TIME* magazine?
   A. On Level 1.　　B. On Level 2.
   C. On Level 3.　　D. On Level 4.

   (4) How much would you have to pay in late fees if you had a book that was 45 days overdue?
   A. $5.50.　　B. $11.00.
   C. $15.00.　　D. $22.50.

   (5) When does the library close on Friday nights?
   A. At 8:30 pm.　　B. At 9:00 pm.
   C. At 9:30 pm.　　D. At 10:00 pm.

🔊 **2. Listen to the talk again and complete the following talk by filling in the words you get from the talk.**

Hello and welcome to the (1)_____ library. This (2)_____ tour will introduce you to our library's facilities and operating hours. First of all, the library's (3)_____ of books, reference materials, and other resources are found on levels one to four of this building. Level One houses our humanities and map collections. On Level Two, you will find our circulation (4)_____, current periodicals and journals, and our copy facilities. Our (5)_____ and engineering sections can be found on Level Three. You can also find back issues of periodicals and journals older than six months on this level. Finally, group (6)_____ rooms, our microfilm collection, and the multimedia center are located on Level Four.

Undergraduate students can check out up to five books for two weeks. Graduate students can check out fifteen books for two months. Books can be (7)_____ up to two times. There is a 50-cent-a-day late (8)_____ for overdue books up to a (9)_____ of $15.00. Periodicals and reference books cannot be checked out.

The library is open (10)_____, 8:00 am to 10:00 pm, and on Saturdays from 9:00 am to 8:30 pm. The library is closed on Sundays.

III. Post-listening exercises

More and more students are using the Internet for conducting research versus going to the library. However, what are the advantages and disadvantages of both? For example, how can you verify the accuracy of information on the Internet? Then, discuss what two things could be added to your own school library to make it more accessible (useful) for international students.

4.2.2 Traffic ticket

Helpful tips

Be aware of the speed limits for different areas in your city and area even if the limits are not posted. Ignorance is no excuse when you are trying to fight a speeding ticket.

I. Pre-listening exercises

What are common traffic violations and how do they threaten public safety (for example, following cars too closely, or tailgating, can result in rear end collisions if the car in front of you stops suddenly)?

II. Listening exercises

1. Listen to the conversation and check your comprehension by choosing the best answer.

(1) What law did the driver break in the school zone?

A. He didn't yield to children when crossing the road.

B. He parked illegally near the school.

C. He exceeded the speed limit.

(2) What happened at the intersection?

A. The driver didn't use his turn signals.

B. The driver didn't come to a complete stop.

C. The driver failed to yield to other drivers.

(3) What did the police officer tell the man about his driver's license?

A. The license was no longer valid.

B. The driver was using someone else's license.

C. The license was only good for 6 more months.

(4) What can be implied from the driver's conversation about the officer's name?

A. The driver planned to report the officer to his superiors.

B. The driver told the officer that they had met before.

C. The driver hinted that the officer could let him off.

(5) What happened at the end of the conversation?

A. The driver got a ticket.

B. The officer arrested the driver.

C. The driver was taken to court.

2. Listen to the conversation again. Complete the conversation by filling in the missing words.

Police Officer: Okay. May I see your driver's license please?

Driver: What? Did I do anything wrong?

Police Officer: License, please. And your car (1) _____.

Driver: Oh, yeah. It's here somewhere in the glove compartment. Yeah, here it is.

Police Officer: Sir, did you realize you were (2) _____ in a school zone?

Driver: What? No, I didn't, but that's probably because my (3) _____ is broken, I mean, malfunctioning.

Police Officer: Yes, you were going 50 miles per hour in a 20-mile per hour zone. And [What?], you failed to come to a complete stop at the (4) _____ back there.

Driver: Rolling stops don't count?

Police Officer: And, one of your break lights is out, [Huh?], you're not wearing a seat belt, and your driver's license (5) _____ six months ago.

Driver: And your name is ... Officer Smith? Hey, are you (6) _____ to the Smiths in town? My wife's cousin's husband (I think his name is Fred) works for the police department here. Or was that the (7) _____ department. Anyway, I thought you might be good pals, and you know ...

Police Officer: Hey, are you trying to (8) _____ an officer? I could have this car impounded right now because of these (9) _____.

Driver: No, of course not.

Police Officer: Okay, then. Here's your ticket. You can either appear in court to pay the (10) _____ or mail it in. Have a nice day.

Driver: Do you take cash?

III. Post-listening exercises

- In your own words, give a summary of the traffic violations the driver in this conversation committed.
- What steps can law enforcement (police officers) take to protect the public and roads in such cases?
- Is it better to try to talk your way out of traffic ticket or just accept the consequences if you have broken a traffic law?

IV. Online investigations

Getting a traffic ticket for different violations can happen if you aren't aware of the laws or code where you live or visit. Choose a country you want to visit and find out about three specific traffic laws and the penalties for violating those laws. How do these rules compare to those in your own area? Keep in mind that the traffic code can vary widely from area to area within the same country. Learning about the criminal justice system before you travel to a new place can help you avoid legal problems.

4.2.3 Smart phones

In today's world, is a phone a necessity for people of all ages, or is it just a luxury item? Why or why not? How do people who grew up without mobile phones feel about this?

Helpful tips

Although texting is a very popular form of communication for short messages, talking on the phone can be even better when you want to avoid misunderstandings on important topics.

I. Listening exercises

🔊 **1. Listen to the conversation and choose the best answer to the statements.**

(1) The young man says he needs a new phone because _____.
   A. his parents took his last one
   B. someone stole his last one
   C. his phone is an older model

(2) How many phones does the young man already have?
   A. Two.
   B. Three.
   C. Four.

(3) According to the conversation, what are the young man's parents like?
   A. Friendly.
   B. Generous.
   C. Kind.

(4) What do the young man's parents want him to do to get a phone?
   A. Take out money from his bank account.
   B. Find a job and work to earn money.
   C. Ask his brother if he can use an old phone.

(5) What is the BEST word to describe the young man's personality?
   A. Talkative.
   B. Mean.
   C. Self-centered.

🔊 **2. Listen to the conversation again and finish the following sentences by filling in words or phrases according to the conversation.**

Please don't (1) _____ when I am talking. We need to discuss the problem about your phone.

Jessica is so (2) _____. She helps anyone who is in need.

Why do you always feel so (3) _____? Do you think it is my responsibility to pay for everything you want?

James need to be more (4) _____ and not depend on help from Mom and Dad.

Be sure to clean the table. I don't want to see even (5) _____ on it.

Module 4 Review

II. Post-listening exercises

Many teachers have concerns about students' use of cell phones at school and in the classroom. Think of three reasons for and against this issue and explain your ideas from your own experience.

Reasons

(1) _____

(2) _____

(3) _____

4.3 Communication bank

Making suggestions

I think you should ...

I don't think you should ...

Why don't you ...

Why don't we ... (do something together)

Let's ...

Match the expressions on the left to the responses on the right.

(1) I think you should buy the blue one.	**A.** Thanks, but I've already been there.
(2) I don't think you should sell your car.	**B.** Sounds like a good idea. Where do you want to go?
(3) Let's go bowling tonight.	**C.** Thanks for the advice, but I really need the money.
(4) Why don't we go skiing on Saturday?	**D.** That's a good idea.
(5) Why don't you come with me to China?	**E.** Sorry, I can't. I'm meeting a friend for dinner.

Sample conversations

(1) A: Should I buy the Porsche or the Ferrari?

B: I think you should buy the Ferrari.

A: Why is that?

B: Because I'd like to borrow it.

(2) A: Why don't you give Daphne a call?

B: Good idea. I haven't seen her for a while.

A: Maybe you should ask her out.

B: Hmmm. I'll think about it.

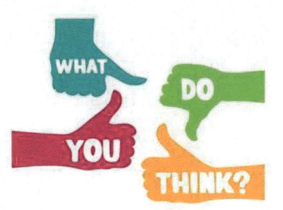

Asking for directions & giving directions

Where is (the) ...? (This is also used in asking about locations.)

How do you get to (the) ... (from here)?

How do I get to (the) ...?

Can you tell me how to get to (the) ...?

Can you give me directions to (the) ...?

What's the best way to get to (the) ...?

Sample conversations

(1) A: Excuse me, is there a grocery store around here?

B: Yeah. There's one right across the street.

(2) A: Can you tell me how to get to Phoenix?

B: Sorry. I don't live around here.

(3) A: Where's Tanner's Leather Shop?

B: It's on the corner of Holly and Vine. Next to the library.

(4) A: How do you get to the bank?

B: Go straight down this street for two blocks. Turn left when you get to Maple Street. Stay on Maple for half a block. It's on the left hand side.

Module 5 Travel

- You and your roommates are going to travel next week.
- Do you know how to reserve a hotel room?
- Do you know how to book a flight?
- Do you know how to pack ?

Module 5 Travel

5.1 Listening and speaking

5.1.1 Deciding where to go

1. Work in pairs and discuss which destination to choose in holidays.

Jiuzhaigou Valley is a nature reserve and national park located in the northern part of Sichuan Province. It is known for its crystal lakes, multi-leveled waterfalls, colorful forests, snow-capped peaks and Tibetan culture.

Kanas, in a valley in the Altai Mountains, is located near the very northern tip of Xinjiang Uygur Autonomous Region. "Kanas" is a Mongolian word meaning "lake in the canyon". The area is famous for its mysterious and wild landscape and especially its legendary lake.

Nyingchi, which means "sun throne" in Tibetan, is situated in the southeast of Tibet. Located in the lower reaches of Yarlung Zangbo River, Nyingchi is blessed with a semi-humid climate and fascinating scenery. It is nicknamed the "Switzerland of Tibet".

Erguna is a wetland area straddling the China-Russian border in the northeast of Inner Mongolia. It is located on the west side of the north of the Greater Xing'an Mountains, which are famed for their stunningly colorful autumn scenery.

73

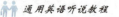

2. Match the English terms [（1）-（10）] with the corresponding definitions.

（1） check-in desk （　） an extended weekend holiday including Friday or Monday
（2） departure lounge （　） you have to show this when you leave and enter different countries
（3） holiday destination （　） a mark made in your passport that allows you to enter a country
（4） long weekend （　） the place where you register for your flight and deposit your luggage
（5） pack （　） a cheap form of accommodation
（6） passport （　） something you buy which makes you think of the place you went to
（7） souvenir （　） a shop that specializes in booking holidays
（8） travel agent （　） where you wait for your flight to be called
（9） visa （　） where you go for a holiday
（10） youth hostel （　） to put your clothes and other things into bags before you go on

3. Practice: Work on your own and make sentences by using the following terms.

（1） check-in desk
（2） departure lounge
（3） holiday destination
（4） long weekend
（5） pack
（6） passport
（7） souvenir
（8） travel agent
（9） visa
（10） youth hostel

5.1.2 Package tour vs independent travel

Group discussion

Here are some pros and cons of package tour and independent travel. Discuss in pairs and put them in corresponding tables. Then add more pros and cons according to your own experience.

- No language problems.
- Choose whatever you want to see.
- May dislike traveling companions.
- Only visit most popular sights.
- Guide explains everything.
- Go at your own pace.
- Need to research beforehand.
- Need to book your own hotels.
- See a lot in a short time.
- Arrange yourself.
- Compulsory "shopping stops".
- No help at hand if you get into difficulties.

Cultural notes

Package tour: A holiday at a fixed price in which the travel company arranges your travel, hotels and sometimes meals for you.

Independent travel: Travel in which you organize things yourself rather than using a company who will arrange flights, hotels, etc.

Package tour		Independent travel	
Pros	Cons	Pros	Cons

Pair work

Suppose you are going to visit Beijing and Singapore. Discuss with your partner and decide whether to travel independently or to take a package tour for each destination.

Package tour
Pros:
_____
_____
_____
_____

Cons:
_____
_____
_____
_____
_____

Independent travel
Pros:
_____
_____
_____
_____

Cons:
_____
_____
_____
_____
_____

Module 5 Travel

5.1.3 Reserving a hotel room

🔊 *1. Listen to the dialogue. Write in the missing words.*

Reserving a hotel room

Date: _____

Name: _____

Price: _____

Type of room: _____

Role-play

Student A: hotel receptionist
Student B: guest
Work in pairs and role-play the conversation according to the information above.

Useful expressions

How long will you stay here?
I want to book/reserve a room for tomorrow.
Do you have any vacant double/single rooms?
Sorry sir, there's no double room available.
Does the price include breakfast?

77

5.1.4 Booking a flight

🔊 1. You will hear a man booking a flight on the phone. Listen to the dialogue and choose the best answer for the following questions.

(1) What's the man's destination?
   A. Salt Lake City, the USA.
   B. New York City, the USA.
   C. Helsinki, Finland.
   D. Stockholm, Sweden.

(2) When is the man's departure date?
   A. The twenty-first.
   B. The thirteenth.
   C. The twenty-third.
   D. The third.

(3) What's the flight number for the second half of his journey?
   A. Flight 555.
   B. Flight 90.
   C. Flight 1070.
   D. Flight 830.

(4) How long is the man's layover between flight?
   A. Less than an hour.
   B. Less than two hours.
   C. Less than three hours.
   D. More than three hours.

(5) What request did the man make regarding his flight?
   A. He asked for a specially-prepared dinner.
   B. He wanted an aisle seat.
   C. He requested a bassinet for his baby.
   D. He asked for a seat near the front of the plane.

2. Listen to the dialogue again. Tick out the information given in it and inquire about the missing information.

Discounts for children	
Destination of the flight	
Meals	
Ticket price	
Departure time/ Arrival time	

Useful expressions

I'd like to make a reservation to … （destination）.
You want to go first class or coach?
What about the fare?
What's the departure/ arrival time?
Does the flight include meals?

5.1.5 Holiday travel

1. Listen to the passage. Write in the missing words.

It's hard to avoid traveling over the holidays but the （1）_____ I had last week really takes the cake.

I flew back to Tucson, Arizona, to be with my wife's family, as we do every Christmas. I got to the airport an hour and a half before my （2）_____ , which I thought would be plenty of time. When I got there, though, I saw that the （3）_____ line was out the door. Because it was the holidays, people were traveling with a lot of extra （4）_____. It took twice as long as it normally would to get to the front of the line. When I finally got to the gate, I found out that my flight had been （5）_____. The gate agent was looking for people to（6）_____ give up their seats for a later flight in （7）_____ for a $100 travel voucher. If she didn't get enough volunteers, she would have to bump people from the flight.（8）_____, several people took her up on the（9）_____ and the rest of us（10）_____.

What a hassle! I love the holidays but I don't love holiday travel.

Group discussion

2. Following is a standard packing list. Work in groups and decide what to pack for different destinations. You may add something else if necessary.

Packing list

Clothes
- ☐ Socks and underwear
- ☐ Light jackets or sweaters
- ☐ Casual shirts
- ☐ Pairs of pants or shorts
- ☐ Swimming suit
- ☐ Comfortable shoes

Medication
- ☐ Eye drops
- ☐ Pain relievers
- ☐ First aid kit
- ☐ Motion sickness medicine
- ☐ Prescription medications

Snacks
- ☐ Crackers
- ☐ Candy
- ☐ Energy bars
- ☐ Bottled water

Electronics
- ☐ Phone charger
- ☐ Camera and charger
- ☐ Music player or e-reader

Toiletries
- ☐ Travel-sized soap, shampoo, toothpaste, etc.
- ☐ Contact lenses or eyeglasses
- ☐ Hand sanitizer
- ☐ Toothbrush
- ☐ Razor
- ☐ Cosmetics/Cologne

Miscellaneous
- ☐ Umbrella
- ☐ Travel guides
- ☐ Area maps
- ☐ Driver's license or identification

Module 5 Travel

Destination A: Hawaii

Packing List

Clothes

Medication

Snacks

Electronics

Toiletries

Miscellaneous

Destination B: Finland

Packing List

Clothes

Medication

Snacks

Electronics

Toiletries

Miscellaneous

5.1.6 At the airport

Pair work

1. Discuss with your partner and put the following conversations into the correct order.

Conversation 1

( ) Yes, this suitcase.
( ) Good morning. Can I see your passport and ticket, please?
( ) Thank you. Goodbye.
( ) Do you have any luggage to check? Please put it on this scale.
( ) Here you are.
( ) Here is your boarding pass. Your boarding time is 11 am.

Conversation 2

( ) Where is seat 36J?
( ) Here you are.
( ) Just go straight and it's on the right.
( ) Please make sure your seat belt is fastened.
( ) Boarding pass, please.
( ) OK.

Role-play

2. Work in pairs and role-play the above conversations.

5.2 Critical thinking and speaking

Task 1

Rubbish island

Watch a video. Write in the missing words.

The Maldives is promoted as a holiday destination with (1) _____ sun, sand and sea. But there's an environmental cost to tourism. Among the country's pristine islands there's also one known as Rubbish Island. (2) _____ are now trying to clean up its image.

Around one million tourists flock to the Maldives each year. It's a country made up of more than one thousand pristine islands. But close to the capital Male there is one place no visitor would want to go. For 20 years Thilafushi — or Rubbish Island — has been the nation's main dumping ground. It's an eyesore but also a serious (3) _____.

"All this garbage, the most serious stuff comes from electronic waste. These things are also burned or buried with the normal waste. Here we are filling the sea, a shallow area, and this garbage is being (4) _____ in the ocean, in liquid. So it's very easy for the heavy metals, the chemicals like lead and all the non-biodegradables to get into the ocean, into the reef around and then into the food chain," said Ali Rilwan, Environmentalist, Bluepeace Maldives.

More than 200 tons of rubbish are dumped on the island every day. Most is from Male but a quarter comes from the nation's holiday resorts. Dozens of (5) _____ workers sift through it separating what to bury from what can be burned.

"When they dump the waste, we find all the plastic items like (6) _____ and put them to one side, then everything else we pile together and set it on fire," said Mohamed DhulaDheen, worker from Bangladesh.

Local (7) _____ plan to stop toxic open burning and build a cleaner incinerator on the island. They also want to reclaim land and move from seafill to landfill. They hope better waste (8) _____ in Male through door-to-door collection and recycling will further help cut damage to the environment around Thilafushi.

"The island will remain as it is because it's an industrial island and the project that is going ahead will monitor air pollution and also the sea pollution near Thilafushi Island and so (9) _____ by waste will be done for Thilafushi. In fact, if we are reclaiming, we will be doing it in an environmentally-friendly manner," said Ahmed Kareem, City Councillor, Male City.

But political upheaval following a sudden change of government last year has meant plans for the island have stalled. As the country struggles to cope safely with waste of its own, environmentalists are (10) _____ tourists to take their most hazardous rubbish such as batteries home.

The Rubbish Island in Maldives

Questions after a trip

- What is your favorite method of travel at your destination? By train? By bus? By boat? By bicycle? Backpacking?
- What is the best kind of holiday for different ages of people, such as children, teenagers, adults, elderly people?
- Do you prefer hot countries or cool countries when you go on holiday?
- Do you think tourism will harm the earth?

Module 5　Travel

Space tourism

Read the passage and discuss the following questions.

Countdown to space tourism

It's 60 feet（18.3 metres） long, made of lightweight, **fuel-efficient** material and can carry eight people out of this world and back.

The first commercial spaceship was **unveiled** by Sir Richard Branson, who hopes to start passenger trips within two years. The price tag: £130,000（1.4 million *yuan*）.

"In time we hope to get that price down and down and down so that, you know, one day, people can think: 'Shall I take my family on holiday to **the Caribbean** or maybe we should try space travel this year?' That's our aim."

Those that can pay will get the **ultimate** three-hour **thrill ride**. The **spaceship rockets** to 62 miles above the earth's surface. Passengers will feel weightless for up to five minutes before heading down through the atmosphere and **gliding** back to the earth.

Organizers say **some** 300 have already **signed up**. Space, as a tourist destination, may be one step closer.

Word tips

fuel-efficient 省油的
the Caribbean 加勒比海地区
thrill ride 刺激的航行
rocket 用火箭运载
some 差不多
unveiled 揭幕，揭开
ultimate 终极的
spaceship 宇宙飞船
gliding 滑行
sign up 登记

Questions about space tourism

- Will space be an exotic retreat reserved for only the wealthy?
- Would you like to try a space travel if possible?

Assignment

Pair work *You and your roommate are going to visit Thailand next summer holiday. Work in pairs and role-play a conversation in a travel agent.*

Student A: You should try your best to book the cheapest holiday and inquire about the distances, prices, travel times, etc.
Student B: Your task is to sell the most expensive holidays.

Student A
You and your roommate are visiting Thailand next summer holiday. You will be landing in Bangkok. Your destination is Chiang Mai, which is located in the north of Thailand. You have to hire a car. You also want to visit Koh Phi Phi and Phuket, which is located in the south of Thailand.

Student B
You are the travel agent. You can organize all aspects of holiday enquiries. Bangkok to Chiang Mai is 700 km. Travel time is approximately 12 hours by car. Car hire is $50 a day for a Toyota Vios and $75 a day for a Toyota Camry. Chiang Mai to Phuket is 1,200 km. It's too far to drive. Flights from Chiang Mai to Phuket take 1 hour and 20 minutes.

Self-assessment

Module 5 Travel

Review the content covered in this module. How well can you do each of the following?

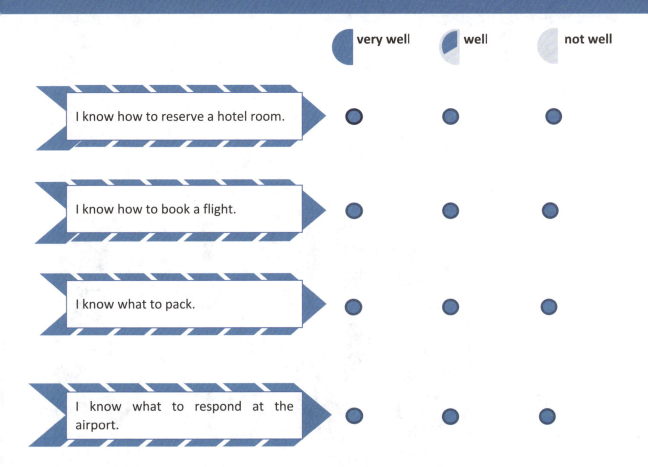

Module 6
Leisure Activities

You and your roommates are planning what to do this weekend.

- Do you know how to talk about your preference?
- Do you know how to describe amusement facilities?
- Do you know how to express your feelings?

Module 6　Leisure Activities

6.1　Listening and speaking

6.1.1　Deciding what to do

1. Fill in the blanks with the given verbs.

play	take	do	go

_____ badminton　　　_____ a bath
_____ nothing　　　　_____ jogging
_____ a nap　　　　　_____ for a drink
_____ some cleaning　_____ yoga
_____ golf　　　　　　_____ out with friends

Pair work

2. Getting together with friends can be fun, especially when you you like hanging out with people. Work in pairs and discuss what kinds of activities you like to do with your friends.

> **Useful expressions**
>
> I quite like ...
> I am crazy about ...
> I am keen on ...
> I couldn't agree with you more.
> You are absolutely right.
> I am afraid I disagree.

🔊 **3. Listen to a dialogue and choose the best answer to the questions.**

（1） What is Sam planning to do with his friends?
　　　A. To have a picnic.
　　　B. To watch a football game.
　　　C. To see a movie and have dinner.
　　　D. To play basketball.

（2） Why does Anna say she can't go with them?
　　　A. She has to prepare for an exam.
　　　B. She can't afford it.
　　　C. She seldom attends a party.
　　　D. She has no interest at all.

（3） What are they planning to do at the end of the evening?
　　　A. To watch a movie.
　　　B. To have a party.
　　　C. To play some games.
　　　D. To play cards.

（4） How is Anna getting to the activity?
　　　A. She's driving her car.
　　　B. Sam is giving her a ride.
　　　C. She's taking the bus.
　　　D. She will walk there.

（5） What time does Anna want to be at home?
　　　A. At 10:30 pm.
　　　B. At 11:30 pm.
　　　C. At midnight.
　　　D. At 10 pm.

Group discussion

4. Imagine that you want to get together with some new friends from out of town next weekend. What two or three leisure or recreational activities. would you consider doing ? Use the Internet to plan your trip and discuss your results.

Leisure activities	Cost	Operating hours	Transportation

6.1.2 Amusement park

1. Match the following amusement facilities with their corresponding words and phrases.

A. Ferris wheel

B. bumper car

C. white water surf

D. corsair

E. roller coaster

F. merry-go-round

2. Listen to the passage. Write in the missing words.

My brother, his wife, and their two daughters are in town and I had promised the girls that I would take them to (1) _____. I don't really like (2) _____, but I knew the kids would like it.

On Saturday morning, we drove down to the theme park. We parked and (3) _____ to the park entrance. We looked at the ticket prices and decided to buy (4) _____ for each of us. Maria, the younger of the two kids, is only 2-year-old, and children under three (5) _____.

The first thing we did was stand in line for the biggest (6) _____ in the park: a really big roller coaster. Actually, only Grace and I (7)_____ since Maria was too young to ride it. My brother and my sister-in-law took Maria to ride the (8) _____ and carousel, and afterwards, we planned to meet near the concession stands so we could watch the (9)_____ at 2 o'clock. Grace and I finally made it to the head of the line and we got on the ride. I really don't like roller coasters. When we got off, I felt queasy and had to (10) _____ before I could walk again.

All in all, we had a good day at the amusement park. But, it will be long time before I go on a roller coaster again!

Pair work

3. Have you ever been to an amusement park? Which amusement facilities do you like best? Work in pairs and talk about your experience.

Useful expressions

It's amazing.   It's fabulous.
It's fantastic.   I feel like throwing up.
I feel dizzy.   It's the last thing I want to do.

6.1.3 Extreme sports

🔊 **1. Listen to the dialogue and write down the extreme sports referred.**

Extreme sports:
(1) _____
(2) _____
(3) _____
(4) _____

Tips

Extreme sports (also called action sports, aggro sports, or adventure sports) is a popular term for certain activities perceived as having a high level of inherent danger. These activities often involve speed, height, a high level of physical exertion, and highly specialized gear.

🔊 **2. Listen to the dialogue once again and write in the missing words.**

...

B: It is. But for me, it's about pushing myself to the limit.

A: Aren't you afraid of (5) _____?

B: Sure. There's always a (6) _____ of getting hurt, but we don't do these sports (7) _____. It's just for fun. I like trying new stunts and seeing how far we can (8) _____ of the sport. Do you want to come with us sometime?

A: Me? I'm not really the (9) _____ type.

...

3. Listen to the passage and choose the best answer to the questions.

(1) What made bungee jumping popular all over the world?
   A. A history of hundreds of years.
   B. Jumping over a river in England.
   C. Coming to China in 1996.
   D. Jumping off a bridge in Britain.

(2) In which sport do people jump from a plane?
   A. Bungee jumping.
   B. Skydiving.
   C. Skateboarding.
   D. Snowboarding.

(3) Why do people wear "baggy trousers"?
   A. They have many bags on them.
   B. They can hold many things.
   C. They make people move freely.
   D. People wearing them can move fast.

(4) What's the Chinese meaning of the word "parachute"?
   A. 直升机.
   B. 降落伞.
   C. 滑板.
   D. 飞艇.

(5) Why do some people like to do extreme sports?
   A. They're dangerous but exciting.
   B. They're exciting and safe.
   C. They're scary but safe.
   D. They're easy to learn.

Module 6 Leisure Activities

Pair work

4. Work with a partner and discuss the questions below.

（1）Have you ever made a bungee jumping?
    If you have, tell your partner about it.
    If you haven't, do you want to try?
（2）Is bungee jumping popular in your country?
（3）Why are there so many people who are crazy about bungee jumping?

95

6.2 Critical thinking and speaking

Task 1 — Extreme sports in South Africa

South Africa is one of the top destinations for extreme sports. Below are some activities you can enjoy there.

1. Bungee jumping from Bloukrans Bridge

Bloukrans Bungee is known as the tallest bungee from a bridge—216 metres. Not only is it taller than the famous New Zealand Nevis Bungee, it's way cheaper. Situated on the edge of Tsisikama National Park, this bungee cannot be missed.

2. **Abseiling** from the Table Mountain

Cape Town's tallest mountain offers abseiling from it. Attached to a regular-looking rope, you can throw yourself down more than 100 meters.

3. **Shark** cage diving in Gansbaai

Shark cage diving is recently a **controversial** activity in South Africa due to some claims that the sharks are being fed with pieces of meat, making them angry. However, I've done it and I don't regret it. While we were waiting for the sharks for a few hours, a majority of the people got seasick. When I finally got to the water it was freezing, but I was so excited about great white sharks swimming around me that I totally forgot about the cold. For the more adventurous traveler（a bigger budget doesn't hurt either）, I recommend a visit to Aliwal Shoal where you can experience free-water shark diving.

4. Riding an **ostrich** in Oudtshoorn

Not surprisingly, Oudtshoorn, known as the ostrich capital of the world, offers ostrich rides. However, it's only available for those under 75 kg. I have to say that for the sake of the experience it's worth it, although the ride is a bit short and expensive.

5. Crocodile cage diving in Oudtshoorn

Sharks might seem scary but crocodiles are definitely faster! In Cango Wildlife Ranch you can be locked in a metal cage and put in a pool with crocodiles. Maybe I'm weird for saying this but I had the impression that the crocodiles were more afraid of me than I was of them.

Word tips

abseil: v.（登山运动中的）沿绳滑下法
shark: n. 鲨鱼
controversial: adj. 有争议的
Ostrich: n. 鸵鸟

Debate

Work in groups and debate on the topic question: "Shall we try extreme sports?"

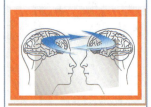

Balancing work and leisure

How to balance our work and leisure activities? And how can we really get the most out of our leisure time without being completely unproductive and lazy?

The first step to this is improving the quality of the activities we currently spend for both work and leisure. By increasing the quality of these activities, we can get a lot more out of them using less time. Too many people watch television shows they have little interest in. Why? Because they don't want to do work and they don't have any better leisure activities that they truly enjoy. Spending some time to really connect with what is important in any situation will allow us to rid ourselves of these time wasters and put it back into things that are truly enjoyable or productive (or both!).

The second issue to solving this problem is energy. Having the time to do things simply isn't enough. Certain tasks require a lot of our focus and energy, usually these tasks are also the same tasks we find most enjoyable or are the most productive. By taking steps to increase our energy levels, through proper diet and exercise, it is easier to focus on these tasks rather than waste time.

By working intelligently, taking actual breaks when you need them instead of just distractions, it will be easier to cut down on the amount of time you spend working. This is because you will be working when you need to work. By cutting down the amount of time you work, you can increase the amount of time you have to enjoy yourself.

The third issue to resolve is in separating your work and leisure time. When you have really motivating goals or a project that make constant demands of your time, it is easy to sacrifice leisure time to continue working. In these cases you feel burnt out and begin to resent the amount of work you have to do.

My solution to this is to guarantee yourself certain blocks of time to leisure. This way you can give yourself plenty of time to enjoy yourself. This allows you to work incredibly hard and really push yourself when you are working, because you know that, no matter what, your work won't creep into your leisure time.

Achieving the balance between work and leisure can be difficult. Understanding that it is not only nice to achieve balance, but absolutely necessary for both our productivity and enjoyment is the first step. Hopefully you can now find your own balance between work and leisure.

Group discussion

For college students, it's not so easy to balance academic study and leisure activities. After reading the passage on Page 97, have you got some good ideas? Work in groups and discuss the best way to balance your study and leisure activities.

Tips

（1）Simply increase the quality of your activities. By working more productively, and spending your leisure time on truly relaxing or enjoyable activities, it is easier to find the time to do both satisfactorily.

（2）Monitor and take control of your energy levels. When you begin to feel drained by a difficult problem at work, take breaks that will really help you take control of your energy levels. Taking proper physical care of your body through diet and exercise is the next step. With more energy, it is easier to increase the quality of our activities.

（3）Ensure that one area of our life doesn't cannibalize the others. Because there is often a great deal of need and urgency attached to work, it is easy to eat away at the leisure time we need to function. In these cases it is often best to guarantee ourselves a certain amount of leisure time in advance.

Assignment

Make a survey among some overseas students and Chinese students. Are there any differences between them in choosing leisure activities? If yes, analyze the results of your survey and make a report on it.

Name	Activities	Name	Activities

Interview sample

The main source of activities, leisure etc. was through the Church of England and the church did very well for me. I joined all the different activities, the Mother's Union, the choir and whatever was going. So, life was not too bad. You had a bit of a social life mixing with the people in church. You were taken out to various places.

My name is Joao Abreu. I came in 1970 from Madeira, Portugal. At the beginning when I came to London, my association was only with a few Portuguese people. Those of my family around here and also some of those I made friends when I was working in the hotel. Then I came to know, even, English people and make friends and of course things started getting better and better and easier for life, because life at the beginning was very difficult, not speaking the language and so on.

New data from the Taking Part survey released today show that more than half of adults in England（53%）had visited a museum or gallery in the last year, maintaining the high reached in 2012/13 and greater than in any previous year.

On top of this 78% of adults had attended or participated in the arts. Heritage also proved a firm favourite with 73% of adults having visited a heritage site. More frequent heritage visitors are also on the increase, 31% visited at least 3-4 times a year.

Furthermore, the national museums in the UK received 4.4 million visits in May 2014 according to figures published today.

Module 6 Leisure Activities

Self-assessment

Review the content covered in this module. How well can you do each of the following?

	very well	well	not well
I know how to talk about my preference.	○	○	○
I know how to describe amusement facilities.	○	○	○
I know how to describe my feelings.	○	○	○
I know how to balance study and leisure activities.	○	○	○

Module 7
Food

Do you know how to book a table?
Do you know how to read a menu?
Do you know how to order a meal?
Do you know how to comment on food?

7.1 Listening and speaking

7.1.1 Deciding what to eat

Today is one of your roommate's birthday. You decide to dine out together. Work in pairs and discuss what to eat to celebrate your roommate's birthday.

Useful expressions

Likes
- I'm fond of/interested in/keen on/crazy about …
- I prefer … to …
- There is nothing I enjoy more than …
- Awesome! / Terrific! / Fabulous!

Dislikes
- I hate/dislike …
- I would rather … than … bore(s)/disgust(s)/me.
- I can't bear/stand/put up with …
- I'm fed up with/tired of …
- … is terrible/awful/disgusting.

7.1.2 Making a reservation in a restaurant

🔊 1. Listen to the conversation and write in the missing information.

Making a reservation

Time: _____

Number of Person: _____

Preference: _____

Name: _____

Useful expressions

Hold the line a moment, please.
I'd like to book a table for four.
We are a group of three.

Just a second, please.
I'd like to make a reservation for …
We'd like to sit in the non-smoking area.

Role-play

2. Work in pairs and role-play the conversation according to the information given on the card. Student A acts as a waiter/waitress. Student B acts as a customer.

Module 7 Food

7.1.3 Reading a restaurant menu

Tips

Knowing how to read a menu, understanding the terminology used and asking the best questions will help ensure you have a top-quality dining experience at the right cost.

1. Match the English menu terms [（1）-（13）] with the corresponding Chinese equivalences （A-M）.

	Terms	Also known as		Chinese equivalences
（1）	appetizers	appies, starters	A.	三明治
（2）	soups	Liquid food	B.	酒水（除水外）
（3）	salads	garden fresh, greens	C.	墨西哥菜
（4）	sandwiches	burgers, from the deli, wraps	D.	意大利菜（意面类）
（5）	Italian	noodles, pasta, pizza	E.	配餐
（6）	main course	main dish, entrée	F.	甜点
（7）	sides	side dishes, accompaniments	G.	儿童菜单
（8）	seafood	fish, fresh from the sea	H.	特色菜
（9）	Mexican	Tex-Mex	I.	汤
（10）	specialties	signature items, favorites	J.	主菜
（11）	desserts	sweets, treats	K.	海鲜
（12）	beverages	drinks, refreshments , liquor, spirits	L.	开胃菜
（13）	kids menu	kids stuff, juniors	M.	沙拉

Cultural notes

A **deli** is a store where you can buy foods（such as meats, cheese, salads, and sandwiches） that are already cooked or prepared.

Mexican（**Tex-Mex**）cuisine is characterized by its heavy use of shredded cheese（切碎的奶酪）, meat（particularly beef and pork）, beans, and spices.

105

🔊 **2. Listen to the passage and take down the four instructions on how to read a menu on the left side of the vertical line in the following T-note.**

Note-taking skills: The T-formation

For a T-formation note, you are supposed to:
（1）Draw a large **T** on a piece of paper. Then, write **the main theme or title** on the top line.
（2）On the left side of the vertical line, write **the basic categories or topics** that have been discussed.
（3）On the right side of the vertical line, write **details, specific examples, follow-up questions or comments**.

Word tips

eatery /ˈiːtəri/
✓ An **eatery** is a place where you can buy and eat food.

Instructions on how to read a menu

（1）Decide_____ you want to eat.	• Courses offered often include:_____,_____, _____, _____ and _____. • Determine how many _____ you wish to order. • Decide which specific _____ you want.
（2）Ask your waiter about any _____.	• _____ or a _____ deal on certain meals. • A prix fixe menu: dishes from a set menu at a _____, often used on _____.
（3）_____.	• Ask any _____ that you do not understand. • You'll know _____ and _____.
（4）Ask about _____.	For example, a restaurant in Boston may _____ freshly caught lobster or clam chowder.

🔊 **3. Listen to the passage again and fill in the missing details on the right side of the vertical line of the table above.**

7.1.4 Asking about dishes on a menu

When asking someone to explain something on the menu, you can use the expressions in bold.

（1） A: Excuse me, **what are** French fries?
　　　B: They are deep-fried potato.
（2） A: **What's in** the Caesar salad?
　　　B: There are lettuce, croutons（油炸面包丁）, cheese, lemon juice, olive oil, eggs, garlic, and black pepper.
（3） A: **Can you tell me what** lasagna（意大利千层面）is, please?
　　　B: It is a noodle pie made with several layers of lasagna sheets, meats, cheeses, and tomato sauce.

Pair work　　Work in pairs. Student A finds the terms on the menu quite new to him. Student B explains the dishes with the given information. Switch roles when practicing.

Ants on the Tree
a stir fried dish; minced pork; glass noodles（粉丝）

Kung Pa Chicken
diced chicken cubes; chili and peanuts

Note
When you explain a dish, you may introduce factors like ingredients, seasonings and ways of cooking.

Buddha-jumping-off-the-wall
broth（汤）; steamed abalone（鲍鱼）; shark's fin（鱼翅）; fish maw（鱼肚）

Borscht
a hot vegetable soup; tomatoes and cubed beef

Word tips

stir-fry 翻炒；煸
cube 切成小块
roast 烘，烤，焙（肉类）
bake （在烤炉里）烘焙
grill （在高温上方或下方）烧烤
toast 烤（尤指面包）
stew 炖，煨
simmer 用文火炖
mash 捣烂，捣碎
mince 用绞肉机绞（食物，尤指肉）
dice 将（肉、菜等）切成小方块，
　　　将……切成丁
shred 切碎，撕碎
steam 蒸（食物）
slice 把……切成薄片

Fuqi Feipian
sliced beef;
ox tripe; chili sauce

Mapo Tofu
hot and soft tofu; minced meet;
a spicy Sichuan peppercorn hot sauce;

7.1.5 Ordering a meal in a restaurant

🔊 *1. You are going to listen to a dialogue between a waiter and a customer. Each time the waiter asks a question, there will be a pause. During the pause please match each question with an appropriate reply.*

Q1	A.	I'd like to have a beef steak.
Q2	B.	Medium, please.
Q3	C.	Yes, I'd like to have a glass of Coke.
Q4	D.	Yes, I'd like to have a bowl of chicken soup, please.
Q5	E.	No, thank you. But I'd like to have the bill, please.
Q6	F.	Yes, please.
Q7	G.	Here, please.

🔊 *2. You will hear a man and a woman ordering a meal in a restaurant. Listen to their conversation and choose the correct answer to each of the following questions.*

（1） What will the man have for a first course?
　　A. Mushroom voulevant.　　　　B. Melon.
　　C. Prawn cocktail.　　　　　　　D. Tomato soup.

（2） What would the woman like for a main course?
　　A. Roast beef with potatoes.　　　B. Roast beef with potatoes and a salad.
　　C. Roast beef with chips.　　　　D. Roast beef with chips and a salad.

（3） What would the man like for a main course?
　　A. Beef with rice.　　　　　　　B. Lamb with a green salad.
　　C. Lamb with rice.　　　　　　　D. Lamb with potatoes.

（4） What will they drink?
　　A. Nothing.　　　　　　　　　　B. Red wine.
　　C. White wine.　　　　　　　　　D. Coffee.

（5） Why can't the woman have the dessert?
　　A. She's got no room.　　　　　　B. She's on a diet.
　　C. She is going to date.　　　　　D. She dislikes the dessert.

（6） What flavor would the man like for his ice-cream?
　　A. Chocolate.　　　　　　　　　B. Vanilla.
　　C. Strawberry .　　　　　　　　　D. Bacon.

3. Listen to a passage about dining in America and mark the following statements T (true) or F (false).

(1) ___ In many American restaurants, the waiters are often very mean and snobbish.
(2) ___ Before the meal gets started, the waiters may introduce themselves and get to know you.
(3) ___ The word entrée means the dessert in North American English.
(4) ___ In North America, typically the customers order an appetizer or starter first, and then a main course and drink.
(5) ___ In English the temperatures of red meat are typically rare, medium, and well done.
(6) ___ It is rude to refuse the suggestions for any extra food made by the waiter.
(7) ___ The customers are usually supposed to tip the waiter 15% to 20% of the bill.

Cultural notes

Did you know …?

American English		British English
appetizer	=	starter
entrée	=	main course
check	=	bill

4. Classify the following expressions into different categories.

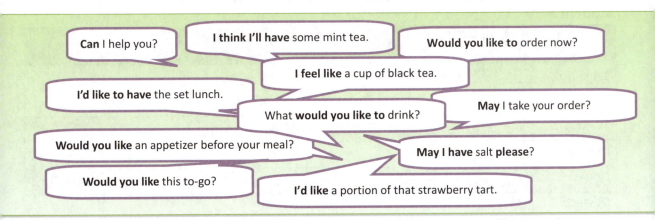

- Can I help you?
- I think I'll have some mint tea.
- Would you like to order now?
- I feel like a cup of black tea.
- I'd like to have the set lunch.
- What would you like to drink?
- May I take your order?
- Would you like an appetizer before your meal?
- May I have salt please?
- Would you like this to-go?
- I'd like a portion of that strawberry tart.

Making offers
Can I help you?
_____
_____
_____
_____

Making requests
May I have salt please?
_____
_____
_____
_____

Role-play

5. Work with your partner and role-play the conservation between a customer and a waiter with the menu and order form printed on Page 111 by using the expressions you have sorted in the boxes above. Remember to cover the following sections in your dialogue.

Waiter	Customer
(1) Greetings	(1) Ask for the specialties or any promotions
(2) Take orders	(2) Ask questions about the terms on the menu
(3) Recommend desserts	(3) Order at least three courses
(4) Confirm orders	(4) Comment on the dishes
(5) Ask about the food	(5) Ask for the bill

Activity cards

Student A

Order form			
Table No.:_____ Persons:_____ Time:_____ Server:_____			
	Dish	Quantity	Special requirements	Price
Starters				
Main courses				
Drinks				
Desserts				
Total				

Student B

Menu

Starters
Soup
Chicken Soup	$12.50
Mushroom Soup	$12.50
Vegetable Soup	$12.50

Bread and Salad
Garlic Bread（3pcs）	$13.00
Smoked Salmon Salad	$18.50
Shrimp & Fresh Fruit Salad	$20.50
Seseme Chicken Salad	$16.50

Main course
Sandwiches
Ham & Cheese Sandwiches	$15.50
Tune & Egg Selad Sandwiches	$16.00

Pizza（1 pc）
Beef, Mushroom & Onion Pizza	$15.00
Chicken & Pork Pizza	$14.50
Vegetarian Pizza	$14.00
Ham, Cheese & Pineapple Pizza	$14.00

Burger
Cheese Burger	$14.50
Beef Burger	$16.00

Pasta
Lasagna	$28.00
Shrimp & Mushroom Spaghetti	$26.00
Super Seafood Spaghetti	$26.00
Chicken Spaghetti	$25.50
Salmon Spaghetti	$25.50

Cold Drinks
Orange Juice	$12
Apple Juice	$12
Lemon Tea	$11
Mincral Water	$7
Soft Drinks—Coke, 7-up,Fanta	$7

Dessert
Red Bean Sundee	$12.00
Vanilla/Chocolate Ice Cream	$10.00
Banana Pancake	$10.00

7.1.6 Food review

🔊 **1. Listen to the short passage and write in the missing words and expressions.**

（1）It was good. The food was _____, but not _____ Italian food at home.
（2）Yeah, I kind of think the same thing. It seemed like the _____ were a little _____, I guess you can say.
（3）Hmm, yeah, _____.
（4）Uh, salad was good, but it's hard to _____ salad.
（5）Yeah, although that salad was pretty nice, right. It was chicken and _____ and _____ and stuff so ...
（6）The pizza was _____. I would like it to be a little bigger because pizza at home is usually much bigger but, it was still very good.

🔊 **2. Listen again and take down the questions you hear in the dialogue.**

（1）
（2）
（3）
（4）
（5）

🔊 **3. Match the words on the left with the correct meanings on the right.**

Descriptive words	Definition
（1）**rich**	A.（food）containing low calories or low amount of sugar, fat or alcohol
（2）**juicy**	B.（food）containing a lot of fat or oil
（3）**crispy**	C. requiring much chewing
（4）**chewy**	D. a strong taste that gives a pleasantly burning feeling in your mouth
（5）**lite**	E. pleasant to smell or taste
（6）**sourish**	F. having the acid taste or smell
（7）**spicy**	G.（food）having a pleasantly hard surface
（8）**savory**	H. having a lot of juice, enjoyable to eat
（9）**fried**	I.（food）that is eaten uncooked, or that has not been cooked enough
（10）**raw**	J. cooked in a pan that contains hot fat or oil

4. Fill in the blanks with the ten words listed above.

（1）I don't like French _____ potatoes because they are not low-calory healthy food.

（2）Additional cream will make the cake too _____.

（3）Vegetables like cabbages and carrots can be eaten _____.

（4）I am still so hungry that I can eat a huge dish of _____ steaming meat.

（5）Compared with chicken soup, I prefer the _____ chicken.

（6）I really like the peach because the flesh is sweet and _____.

（7）My favorite milk product is _____ yogurt.

（8）I can't bear _____ oranges.

（9）The dessert is a (n) _____ cookie made with egg white, sugar and almond paste.

（10）I can't have enough of _____ hot pot.

5. Comment on the meal that you have just taken with your friends or partner.

Useful expressions

- Do you like the appetizer?
- How do you like Italian food?
- What do you think of this Japanese restaurant?
- What do you think about the dessert?
- Is it expensive or cheap?

Your dishes:
_____
_____
_____
_____

Your comment on your dishes:
_____
_____
_____
_____

7.1.7 Rising and falling intonations

An intonation is the music of the language. It is the way how voice rises (goes up) and falls (goes down) in a phrase or sentence.
- In a falling intonation, the voice goes up on the most important word in a phrase or sentence and falls at the end.
- Statements and *Wh*-questions usually end with a falling intonation.
- In a rising intonation, the voice goes up at the end.
- *Yes/No* questions usually end with a rising intonation.

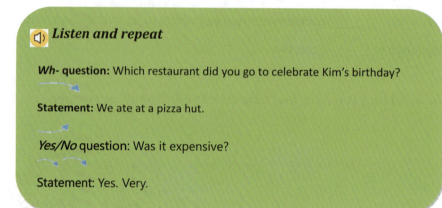

Listen and repeat

Wh- question: Which restaurant did you go to celebrate Kim's birthday?

Statement: We ate at a pizza hut.

Yes/No question: Was it expensive?

Statement: Yes. Very.

Read the following dialogues with your partner, using correct rising and falling intonations.

(1) — Good morning, Madam. Can I take your order now?
— Yes, please.

(2) — Would you like to have a starter?
— Yes, I'd like to have a bowl of chicken soup, please.

(3) — How would you like your steak cooked?
— Medium, please.

Module 7 Food

7.2 Critical thinking and speaking

Task 1

Healthy food or junk food?

Pair work

1. How many of these statements are true to you? Check true or false, and then discuss with your partner.

- ◆ Kids need to drink cow's milk. ☐
- ◆ It's easy to exercise off extra calories. ☐
- ◆ It's essential to drink eight glasses of water a day. ☐
- ◆ Soy products cause cancer. ☐
- ◆ Olive oil is "good" fat. ☐
- ◆ A glass of wine every day promotes good health. ☐
- ◆ The more protein you eat the better. ☐
- ◆ Fish is the best brain food. ☐
- ◆ Orange juice and milk should never be drunk together. ☐

> **Discussion**
>
> 2. What food is necessary for our daily life? Read the following pyramid and you may find something useful.

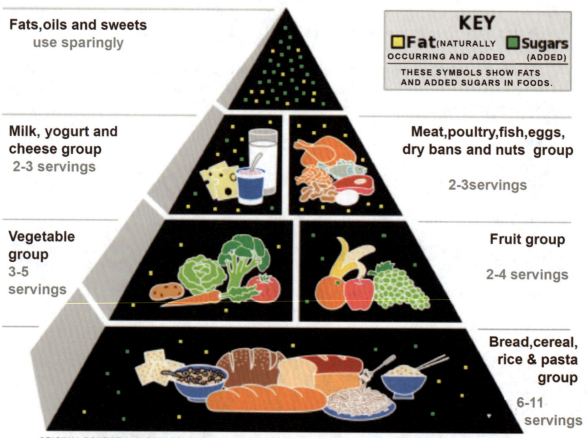

Pair work

3. What is junk food? What is healthy food? Classify the following food into junk food and healthy food.

Pair work

4. Try to list some key features of both junk food and healthy food. Then classify the following words into the table below and discuss with your partner.

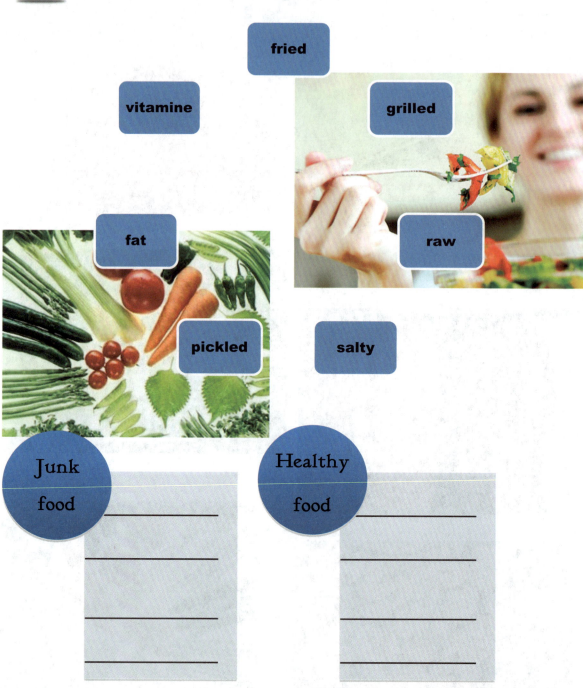

fried

vitamine

grilled

fat

raw

pickled

salty

Junk food _____
_____
_____
_____
_____

Healthy food _____
_____
_____
_____
_____

Module 7 Food

Task 2

Shall we say "no" to junk food?

Group work

Read the following views from three different speakers. Work with your group members to justify your answers to the question :"Shall we say 'no' to junk food?"

Points of view A

Junk food is consumed by all classes of people. It is not the patent of the poor. Some kinds of junk food is also expensive.

Points of view B

You said the high tax may lead the bankruptcy of the factories, which may result in job loss. These factories producing junk food will be closed while the factories producing healthy food will boom.

Points of view C

The workers who work for the junk food companies will be dismissed. But the factories producing healthy food will expand their employees. So people can still get a job.

119

You are what you eat

Depending on what you want from your body, you must put in it the right food. You need to pay special attention to what you eat. That's right: Your shopping list can help with your to-do list. That's because the right foods are a kind of clean-burning fuel for your body's biggest energy hog/pig: Your brain.

Stock up on these items to, jog your memory, sharpen your senses, improve your performance, activate your feel-good hormones, and protect your quick-witted sharpness, whether you're 15 or 40 years old.

Water: The body's most important nutrient

One should drink at least 2 liters water per day, and if you exercise or are overweight, even more. Your blood is approximately 90% water and is responsible for transporting nutrients and energy to muscles and for taking waste from tissues.

For short-term memory: Drink coffee

Fresh-brewed coffee is the ultimate brain fuel. Caffeine has been shown to retard/slow the aging process and enhance short-term memory performance.

For long-term memory: Eat blueberries

Antioxidants in blueberries help protect the brain from free-radical damage and cut your risk of Alzheimer's and Parkinson's diseases when you get older. They can also improve cognitive processing （translation thinking）.

To think faster: Eat salmon or mackerel

So put salmon or mackerel on the grocery list. The omega-3 fatty acids found in fatty fishes are a primary/major building block of brain tissue, so they'll boost up your thinking power. Salmon is also rich in niacin, which can help ward off Alzheimer's disease and slow the rate of ageing.

Assignment

Read the passage on the left and discuss with your group members:

（1）Do you agree with the suggestions in the passage? Why or why not?

（2）Work with your group members and try to find out more helpful food in our life and give a mini-presentation of about 2 minutes in next class.（You may use the sentence patterns in this passage as reference.）

Self-assessment

Review the content covered in this module. How well can you do each of the following?

	very well	well	not well
I know how to book a table.	●	○	○
I know how to read a menu.	○	○	○
I know how to order a meal in a restaurant.	○	○	○
I know how to comment on food.	○	○	○

Module 8 Review

| Group discussion skills | Further listening and speaking | Communication bank |

8.1 Group discussion skills

8.1.1 Group discussion and its skills

A group discussion, or GD, is a collective combination of available information. Each individual in the group is believed to have a say in the process of communication.

Why have discussion?

- To understand a subject or topic area more deeply.
- To explore ideas and exchange information.
- To improve your ability to think critically.
- To improve your language skills.
- To increase your confidence in speaking.
- To help a group make a particular decision or come to a conclusion.

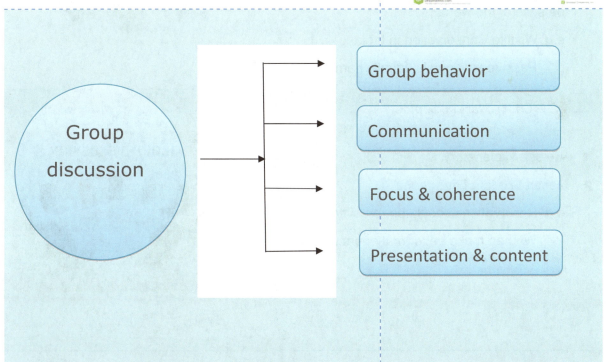

3 topic types of GD

- Factual topics

- Controversial topics

- Abstract topics

（1）Factual topics

- As the word says—about facts
- Test how much you know, how much you are aware of the various things happening around you and of the state of the world

  e.g. Wildlife Conservation in India

       Passive smoking is equally harmful.

（2）Controversial topics

- Are self-explanatory
- Generate a lot of argument

  e.g. Reservations should be removed.

       Women make better managers.

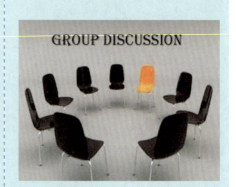

(3) Abstract topics

- Things that cannot be touched, not be easily defined or formulated
- Test your lateral thinking and creativity
  e.g. vegetarianism, political correctness

5 strategies for improving discussion skills

If you find it difficult to speak or ask questions in tutorials and seminars, try the following strategies.

- Observe
- Learn to listen
- Prepare
- Practice
- Participate

(1) Observe

Attend as many GDs as possible and notice what other people do. Ask yourself:

- How do others enter into the discussion?
- How do they ask questions?
- How do they disagree with or support the topic?
- How do other students make critical comments?
- How do they signal to ask a question or make a point?

（2）Learn to listen

Listening is an essential skill and an important element of any discussion. Effective listeners don't just hear what is being said, but they think about it and actively process it.

- Be an active listener and don't let your attention drift.
- Identify the main ideas being discussed.
- Evaluate what is being said. Think about how it relates to the main idea/ theme of the discussion.
- Listen with an open mind and be receptive to new ideas and points of view.
- Take notes about things to which you could respond.

（3）Prepare

You can't contribute to a discussion unless you are well-prepared. Make sure you are clear about the discussion topics and complete any assigned reading materials.

（4）Practice

Practice discussing assigned topics and materials outside class. Start in an informal setting with another student or with a small group. Begin by asking questions of fellow students. Ask them about:

- the course material
- their opinions
- information or advice about the course

Practice listening and responding to what they say. Try out any discipline-specific vocabulary or concepts.

Becoming accustomed to expressing your views outside class will help you develop skills you can take into the more formal environment.

(5) Participate

An easy way to participate is to add to the existing discussion. Start by making small contributions:

- agree with what someone has said
- ask them to expand on their point（ask for an example or for more information）
- prepare a question to ask beforehand

You can then work up to:

- answering a question put to the group
- providing an example for a point under discussion
- disagreeing with a point

1 Leader

Leadership is all about giving directions to the group in terms of content in GD. It is about initiating the discussion and suggesting a path on which the group can continue the discussion.

A good leader is one who allows others to express their views and channels the discussion to a probable decision or conclusion on the given topic.

Signal words in talk

Voicing an opinion

1. A valid opinion

I believe that ...

I think that ...

From what I understand ...

As I understand it ...

2. A reason why

This is due to ...

Because ...

What I mean by this is ...

3. Evidence

For instance ...

For example ...

An example can be seen ...

（Author's name）states that ...

Statistics from（give a source）indicate ...

Arguing a point: How to disagree effectively

1. Acknowledge their point

I can see your point, however ...

That's a good point, but ...

I see what you're getting at, but ...

2. Explain why you disagree

That's not always the case because ...

That's not necessarily true because ...

This idea isn't supported by statistics/evidence ...

I thought the author meant that ...

3. Offer your opinion completely with reason

Module 8　Review

Support

1. A valid opinion

From what I've read ...

The statistics seem to show that ...

I think what the author may actually be suggesting is ...

Other studies by author/report show that ...

Now, be prepared for counter-argument and further discussion!

8.1.2　Group discussion practice

I. Pre-listening exercises

Work in pairs and discuss the following questing.

（1）How often do you read a book?

（2）How is a book different from other media?

II. Listening exercises

🔊 *Listen to the talk. Write in the missing expressions.*

Facebook boss Mark Zuckerberg (1) _____ what could be the world's largest book club. Zuckerberg said last week that his (2) _____ was to read a book (3) _____. He invited his 30 million followers to join him (4) _____. He created a Facebook page called A Year of Books, on which he announces what his latest read is and asks people to discuss the book with him. He explained: "I've found reading books very (5) _____. Books allow you to fully explore a topic and (6) _____ in a deeper way than most media today."

Zuckerberg already has his first book, "The End of Power" by Moises Naim. He explained: "It's a book that (7) _____ how the world is shifting to give individual people more power that was (8) _____ by large governments, militaries and other organizations. The trend towards giving people more power is one I believe in deeply." Zuckerberg takes on a challenge every year as a way (9) _____ of thinking and learn more about the world, different cultures, beliefs, histories and technologies. An (10) _____ was to learn to speak Mandarin, which he did.

III. Post-listening exercises

Today more people are reading e-books instead of paper books. Another trend is that various kinds of media are distracting people from reading paper pages. Discuss the following questions in your group, with one student leading the discussion.

(1) Which do you prefer, books or other media, when you try to get to explore a certain topic? Why?

(2) Do you think paper books will one day be completely replaced by electronic media? Why?

8.2 Further listening and speaking

8.2.1 Travel peak: Chinese National Day

I. Pre-listening exercises

Work in pairs and discuss the following questions.

Chinese National Day is usually a travel peak for its people. For tourists, travel is about enjoying their visit and having a good time. But do you know what National Day is for cleaners?

II. Listening exercises

Listen to the talk. Write in the missing words.

Cleaners in tourist spots across the country have their work cut out due to the increase in tourist numbers. But some of these tourist spots have now come up with (1) _____ ways to reduce the workload for these cleaners.

For tourists, travel is about enjoying their visits and having a good time. But for cleaners, it is something else entirely. The National Day holiday travel peak means a lot more work.

Take for instance Gulangyu Island in Xiamen, east China. Authorities (2) _____ during this holiday period, around 60 thousand tourists will travel there every day.

That number can fill a garbage bin every 20 minutes, doubling the workload for cleaners on the island.

"The bin weighs around 15 kilograms. It gets full every 20 minutes," Yang Shunyu, a cleaner said.

Though the increased workload is (3) _____ for him, Yang tells us there are a number of tourists who are helpful and make the job easier for him.

But not all tourists are this (4) _____, which is why, Xi'an City in northwest China has come up with a (5) _____ plan to reduce the workload for its cleaners. Here, tourists can exchange an empty plastic bottle or any garbage, for a free bottle of water.

Naturally, tourists are a happy (6) _____.

Last year, around a million tourists visited Lintong district in Xi'an during the National Day holiday. They left behind a huge mess at scenic spots to clean up.

So, the local authority came up with the idea of exchanging garbage for water.

"Garbage thrown on the ground can be cleaned ... but when people leave garbage on the mountain in the forest park, it is (7) _____. Cleaning up the mountain puts us under (8) _____ pressure," Han Zhao, Director of Civilization Office of Lintong, Xi'an said.

Hubei Province in central China has gone even further. Tourists in Shi'en Canyon can now exchange half a kilo of garbage for a free ticket of the Dragon-boat (9) _____ show.

"I saw a poster on the ticket box that Shi'en Canyon now offers a free show ticket in exchange for half a kilogram of garbage. So I brought my child to help. I want her to learn about protecting the environment," a tourist said.

Local authorities say that for environment protection to succeed, society needs to get involved as a whole. They also say that they want to promote the idea of (10) _____ travel for all people in the country.

III. Post-listening exercises

What do you think of littering? If you see someone litter, will you try to stop them from doing that? Discuss in group and find out what you can do to reduce and stop littering among tourists.

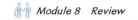

8.2.2 Health benefits of having hobbies and leisure activities

I. Pre-listening exercises

Work in pairs and discuss the following questions.

Is it only fun to have leisure activities to the elderly? Besides refreshing the mind and body, do you think there might be some health benefits if they are active in certain activities?

II. Listening exercises

🔊 *Listen to the talk. Write in the missing words.*

Beneficial factors	Details	Example
Enhance the (1)_____ system	(2)_____ activity can help prevent or maintain control in some (3)_____ illnesses such as heart disease, diabetes, arthritis, and even some types of cancer.	Exercising, playing games, horseshoes, golf, (4)_____, or basketball
Improve (5)_____	Moving can assist in stretching (6)_____ _____.	Walking, (7)_____, stretching, swimming, painting, Tai Chi or dancing
Improve memory	Many hobbies will challenge your mental abilities and enhance your problem-solving skills.	Word searches, crossword puzzles, brain games, sudoku, or card games
Reduce stress	Some of these ideas may also help create a calm atmosphere to reduce stress.	Cooking or baking, gardening, taking a walk, singing, reading, or playing a (8)_____
Improve (9)_____	Some hobbies even involve other people which can creat social opportunities and ...	Card games, board games, shopping, knitting, or scrapbooking
Better quality sleep	Being more active during the day helps create a more (10)_____ night's sleep.	/

III. Post-listening exercises

- Work in pairs to review the health benefits of having leisure activities and hobbies.
- Follow the example of the passage to work out some possible benefits of having leisure activities to college students by giving the **beneficial factors**, **details** and **examples**.
- Will you try some new activities, such as travelling in a hot-air balloon?

8.2.3 Where to serve the dishes on a table

I. Pre-listening exercises

There are several aspects of differences between Chinese dinner and western dinner including dinner procedure, dinner instruments, ways of serving, structure of dishes etc. Do you happen to notice the differences of the position on a table where dishes are served between Chinese dinner and western dinner?

II. Listening exercises

🔊 *Listen to the talk and answer the following questions.*

（1）Where are dishes served on the table in western dinner?

_____

（2）Where are dishes served on the table in Chinese dinner?

_____

（3）How are staples like rice served in Chinese dinner?

_____

（4）Why is the Chinese way of having dinner helpful when several people go out for dinner?

_____

（5）Why do Chinese restaurants in western countries cut off some dishes from the menus?

_____

III. Post-listening exercises

Discuss with your partner about where you prefer to serve the dishes, at the center of the table or in each one's plate. Then you will decide together about the pros and cons of each different way.

Dishes at the center of the table		Dishes in each one's plate	
Pros	Cons	Pros	Cons

Module 8 Review

8.3 Communication bank

Useful expressions

Making reservations for a room

I want to book/reserve a room for tomorrow.

Do you have any vacant double/ single rooms?

Does the price include breakfast?

How much is the charge per night?

I'll be arriving on ...

1. Match the expressions on the left to the responses on the right.

(1) Royal Inn. How may I help you?	A. Two nights. I'll be leaving on June 17.
(2) Certainly, sir. When will you be arriving?	B. Hello, I'd like to reserve a single room for next week.
(3) How many nights will you be staying?	C. Thanks.
(4) I'll check to see if there are any vacancies. Please hold on.	D. Well, I'll be arriving on June 15.
(5) Hello, sir. There are rooms available on June 15.	E. Great! By the way, what is the room rate?

Sample conversation

Asking for a room at a hotel

Clerk: Good evening. May I help you?

Sam: I need a single room, please.

Clerk: Do you have a reservation?

Sam: No, I'm afraid I don't.

Clerk: How long will you be staying with us?

Sam: Just one night.

Clerk: Would you prefer a non-smoking room?

Sam: Yes, please.

Clerk: OK. We have a single non-smoking room on the 10th floor.

Sam: Great! What's the room rate?

Clerk: US$65 plus tax. Breakfast included.

Sam: Excellent!

Clerk: May I ask you to fill out this form for me, please?

Sam: Sure.

Useful expressions

Expressing likes

I quite like ...	I am crazy about ...
I am keen on ...	I couldn't agree with you more.
You are absolutely right.	I am afraid I disagree.

Sample conversation

A: What a wonderful dinner!

B: Thank you. I am glad you are enjoying it.

A: Where did you get your fantastic recipes?

B: I grew up cooking. My mother shared her recipe with me.

A: I especially like the wonderful chicken dish.

B: That is a special coconut ginger chicken with rice dish.

A: Is that shrimp in the soup?

B: Yes. Do you like it? I added a little extra lemon grass and some sea vegetables.

A: I am happy that the wine I brought for you works well with this meal.

B: Yes, thank you for bringing the wine. It really complements the meal.

Module 9

Job and Career

What is your plan for future job?
What usually occurs when job-hunting?
What are the differences between jobs and career?
What is job satisfaction? How important is it?
What kind of job is most suitable for you?

9.1 Listening and speaking

9.1.1 Career terms

1. Classify the following words into two categories.

| accountant | artist | banker | bookkeeper | builder | butcher | carpenter | chef |
| coach | dentist | designer | doctor | economist | editor | engineer | lawyer |

Job	Career

Module 9 Job and Career

9.1.2 Career search

🔊 *Listen to the following dialogue and finish the multiple choices below.*

(1) What kind of career does the woman want to pursue?
   A. She wants to become a sales associate for an auto company.
   B. She is interested in repairing and maintaining cars and other vehicles.
   C. The woman wants to major in mechanical engineering.

(2) Right now, the woman's boyfriend is _____.
   A. majoring in secondary education
   B. pursuing a career in auto mechanics
   C. getting a degree in a medical field

(3) What does Ryan think about James' future career?
   A. He thinks that there is no money in that profession.
   B. He believes that James isn't qualified for the job.
   C. He feels that James is pursuing a job designed for women.

(4) Ryan suggests that women are more suited for jobs in _____.
   A. education and office work
   B. farming and house cleaning
   C. nursing and child care

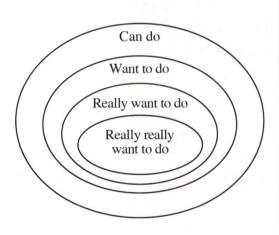

Which career fits?

141

9.1.3 Finding a job

🔊 *Listen to the passage and write in the missing words.*

There are many ways to find a job. It can be as easy as walking into a neighborhood store to look at its (1) _____.

Local stores often have areas where people can put small signs telling what kind of service they need or can provide. Such services include (2) _____ or (3) _____.

Another popular tool for finding jobs is (4) _____. Job searchers can also look in the newspaper. (5) _____ have employment announcements placed by companies seeking workers.

Another useful way to find a job is through (6) _____. For example, students can go to (7) _____ to get help in finding a job. People who graduate from universities can also use (8) _____ and resources. This means that new graduates can get advice about jobs from older graduates.

Each American state also has (9) _____ that can help people train and look for jobs.

9.1.4 Advice on campus life

1. Brainstorm a list of 5 advice topics that you use in your daily life.

Examples: low GPA, broken heart, being late for class, etc.

(1) _____

(2) _____

(3) _____

(4) _____

(5) _____

Asking for advice	Giving advice
• What do you think I should do（about …）？ • What should I do（about …）？ • What would you do（about …）？ • What would you suggest（I do）（I should do about …）？ • Can/Could you give me some advice（about …）？	• Why don't you …? • If I were you, I would … • Maybe you should … • I suggest you … • How about（verb+ing …）？ • You might try（verb+ing …） • My advice would be to … • It might be a good idea to …

Pair work

2. Work in pairs. Use the phrases above to ask for and give advice on the 5 topics listed in Exercise 1.

Example: Low GPA
A: What do you think I should do about my low GPA?
B: Why don't you try harder in class?

9.1.5 How to talk about your job

🔊 *Listen to the talk and take down the meaning of 5 idioms of complaining about your job.*

5 idioms for complaining about your job	Meaning
(1) "My co-workers don't <u>pull their weight</u>, and I'm always picking up the slack."	
(2) "I can't stand the office politics. It seems like <u>kissing up to the people</u> who call the shots is the only way to move up the ranks."	
(3) "My boss loves to micromanage and I can't do my best work when she's constantly <u>breathing down my neck</u>."	
(4) "The job itself is rewarding, but the salary and benefits <u>leave a lot to be desired</u>."	
(5) "I feel like I'm <u>spread too thin</u>, but every time I wrap up one project, I'm given two more—which, of course, need to be done yesterday."	

9.1.6 Do you feel boxed in?

How do you see your present job, as a rigid four equal sided box with no give and take or irregularly shaped which has a certain amount of flexibility?

In other words, first look at changing aspects of your job before changing your position or employer. Here are three things to focus on in job redesign—shaping your job to fit you better.

- **Task content**
  So what changes in your job can you suggest to your boss that will benefit the department and also give you greater job satisfaction?

- **Relationships**
  So how can you modify your job to allow for more interactions with others inside and outside the department and the company?

- **Purpose**
  So how do you see your job? Can you identify how or what you do makes an impact on your boss, your department, the company? Everyone should know and let others know their contributions.

9.1.7 Office party

Warmer

Have you ever been to an office party? What was it like? Do you think it's a good idea to have parties where people work? Does anybody in the class NOT like going to parties or social events with the people you work with?

Background information and guidelines

You have all been invited to an office end-of-the-year party. Each person will have a different role.

The president of the company is not in the role-play. This means that everybody can gossip about work and complain about the president!

Follow these guidelines each time you talk to someone new.

- Introduce yourself and greet the other person.

- Ask some questions to make a small talk.

- Listen to others' gossip and react.

9.2 Critical thinking and speaking

Task 1

Do you "work to live or live to work"?

In a recent Leading News, e-newsletter, from Marshall Goldsmith, the premier executive coach, asked that question. Why? Because if you figured how much time you spent at work—approximately one-third of our waking hours—then you realize that your job has a significant impact on your life.

He created an exercise to help people evaluate their job satisfaction and, most importantly, their career choice. There are three categories and you are to estimate the percentage of your job that falls within each category.

You Try It.

The first category is "play". This is job content that is fun and what you would tend to do regardless of whether or not you were compensated for it. We have all seen people readily agree to do a task that was beyond the job description. Why? Because it was a task they viewed as fun, as an outlet for untapped creativity or a channel for self-development. If I tell myself, "I'm going to play," then there is no resistance or creative avoidance.

The second category is "work". This is job content that is not play. It's work. This is an activity that, although not fun, you would agree to do for reasonable compensation.

The third category is "misery". Job content in this category is not only not play, but it is drudgery, and at times pure hell. And we can find all times of creative reasons to avoid and procrastinate.

How do you see the composition of your work experience concerning activities that are categorized as play, work, and misery? Do you need to write yourself a new job description?

Here are the typical survey results among professionals:

15 percent of what professionals do is considered play;
75 percent of what professionals do is considered work;
10 percent of what professionals do is considered misery.

Group work

Work in groups. Exchange your answer to this question with your group members and try to support your answer by giving examples. 15 minutes later, choose a representative from each group and report to the class.

Task 2

Have you noticed the differences between a job and a career? Which one means much more than the other? What can be done to develop a job into a career?

Differences between job and career

Key Difference: Jobs are often activities that are done in exchange for money. A career is something that a person wishes to have, though it could also be done in exchange for money.

Almost everyone in their lives comes to point of differentiating a job from a career. This point is believed to the key point in a person's life, where they take an active decision of what they want to for the rest of their life. There is a famous quote by Confucius which states, "Choose a job you love, and you will never have to work a day in your life." Many people often confuse a job from a career, believing them to be the same thing as both of them are done in exchange for money.

However, these are two different terms and should not be confused.

Jobs are activities that are performed in exchange for a monetary value. A job is often short-term and only done as a person requires money to live. Jobs do not make a significant impact on society or the person's life and are commonly short-term. If a person is unhappy with a job, they tend to move on to a better one. There are also various different types of jobs including full-time, part-time, seasonal, temporary, odd jobs and self-employment. Jobs also depend on the type. It may require a specialized study. The hours of the job also depend on the type of job it is, which can range from an hour to 9 hours.

Careers are different as they almost always last a life-time. Oxford Dictionary defines "career" as, "course or progress through life（or a distinct portion of life）." This is broader compared to jobs and can also encompass a number of jobs that a person has done in his/her life. It also requires specialized studies, training or formal education to have a career. The term "career" became popular in the late 20th century, when a wide range of choices allowed a person to plan and design a career that he/she may have.

Jobs and careers are different in almost every sense. Where a job is considered just as a person who puts time and energy in return of money, a career is considered as something a person puts his heart and soul into. Jobs are also changeable, where a person who is working as a salesman could be hired as a manager or a CEO. However, a career is something that a person does his whole life, the person would be in management services, which would be a career. Best example for the difference between a job and a career is a doctor. Being a doctor would be the individual's career; however he may have served over 30 hospitals. Each time the doctor changed a hospital, he would change his job, but he would always remain a doctor. Careers are also not specified to providing monetary benefit, if a person wishes to become a volunteer or a social helper, he/she may not always get money for what they do.

Jobs are important in the aspect that a person needs money to live in this world; however careers are what make and break a person as they decide what kind of a person he/she is. They define the person, while a job just defines a post. It is always important to pick a career that a person will truly love, as it is difficult to change it frequently.

	Job	**Career**
Definition	Jobs are often activities that are done in exchange for money.	A career is something that a person wishes to have, though it could also be done in exchange for money.
Require	Depending on the type of jobs it may or may not require extra studies.	Careers most often require a person to take up specialized studies.
Risk	Jobs are considered as safe, where a person does not take risks and just does what he has to in exchange for money.	Careers are something where a person is willing to take risks and willing to exceed for himself and the people he/she is working with.
Time	Jobs are usually short-term, though some people may stick to it because of security.	Careers are usually long-term and often take up half or more of a person's life.
Income	Jobs give employees incomes.	Careers may or may not give employees incomes, depending on the jobs.
Contribution to society	Jobs often contribute little to society only in terms of unemployment and employment rates, along with moving of cash.	Careers contribute high value as social change/progress may be possible.

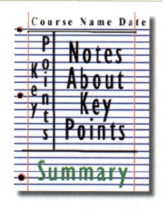

Try to summarize the main differences between jobs and careers by using the format given to you on the left.

Assignment

What do you think might be the possible factors contributing to career searching? Work in pairs. Take turns asking and answering the questions in the Career Aptitude Test. Take short notes on your partner's answers.

Career Aptitude Test </br> *A test can help you decide which job or career is right for you.*	
Interview questions	My partner's answers
（1）Are you a creative person?	
（2）Do you like to explore new places?	
（3）Are you afraid of dangerous situations?	
（4）Do you have good communication skills?	
（5）Do you like reasoning?	
（6）Are you a good problem-solver?	
（7）Do you like to spend time with other people?	
（8）Do you like to help people?	

Group work

Step 1 Tell the group which job might be best for your partner. Explain your reasons.

Step 2 Tell the group your opinion of your partner's choice of a job for you. Is it suitable for you? Why?

Step 3 Try to summarize the main skills or personalities contributing to career planning and give a report in the next class.

Self-assessment

Review the content covered in this module. How well can you do each of the following?

	very well	well	not well
I know how to ask for advice when job-hunting.	○	○	○
I know the main differences between jobs and careers.	○	○	○
I know the main factors to consider when job-hunting.	○	○	○
I know the main differences between work to live and live to work.	○	○	○

Module 10 Volunteer

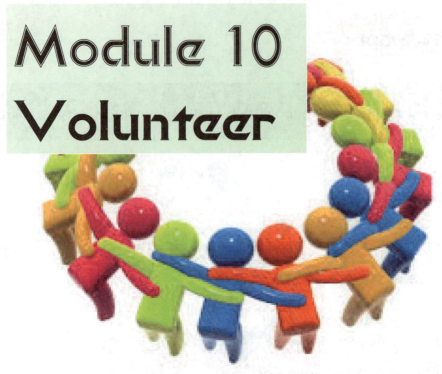

You and your friends are warm-hearted college students who want to volunteer your time and skills.

Do you know International Volunteer Day?

Do you know why volunteer work and organizations are needed?

Do you know the different types of volunteering activities?

Do you know where to volunteer your time?

10.1 Listening and speaking

10.1.1 Volunteer organization

1. Match the picture of logo with the volunteer organization listed below.

☐	British Youth Council	英国青年义工组织
☐	Volunteer Movement	香港福利署义工运动
☐	Volunteer Expo Milano 2015	2015 年米兰世博会志愿者
☐	Volunteer 2008 Beijing Olympic	2008 年北京奥运会志愿者
☐	Volunteer 2010 Guangzhou Asian Game	2010 年广州亚运会志愿者
☐	Volunteer Maldives	马尔代夫公益项目

2. What can you do as a volunteer? Complete the following table and share what you have written with your partner.

For	What can you do?	What will the effect be?
a parent		
a student		
an old person		
your teacher		
a charity		
your city		

10.1.2 International Volunteer Day

🔊 *1. Listen to the passage and number these lines in the correct order.*

(　) There are thousands of volunteer organizations around the world.

(　) Without volunteers, many people around the world would be worse off.

(　) Volunteers help other people and help animals, the countryside, the environment and many more things that are so important to us.

(　) This highly important day was started by the United Nations in 1985.

(　) Some of them are very famous.

(　) A search on the Internet will pretty much give you a volunteer group on anything or anyone you want to help.

(　) The great thing about voluntary work is that it makes you feel like a better person.

(　) Most voluntary work that takes place around the globe is by individuals helping their neighbours.

(　) December 5th is International Volunteer Day.

2. Listen to the passage again and fill in the blanks with what you hear.

Come on everybody. Get up and do something. December 5th is International Volunteer Day. This highly important day was started by the United Nations in 1985. Its (1) _____ _____ is **twofold:** First, to thank volunteers around the world for giving their time to help others; and second, to (2) _____ other people to do voluntary work. Without volunteers, many people around the world would be worse off. In fact, the whole world would be a (3) _____ place. Volunteers help other people and help animals, the countryside, the environment and many more things that are so important to us. The UN urges governments around the world to (4) _____ measures to (5) _____ awareness of the important contribution of volunteering.

There are thousands of volunteer organizations around the world. Some of them are very (6) _____. Perhaps everyone has heard of VSO (Voluntary Services **Overseas**), the Peace Corps, and Muslim Aid. A search on the Internet will pretty much give you a volunteer group on anything or anyone you want to help. You don't need to (7) _____ a **worldwide** group to be a volunteer. Most voluntary work that takes place around the globe is by individuals helping their neighbours. We have probably all (8) _____ out of our way to help someone (9) _____ fortunate. The great thing about voluntary work is that it makes you feel like a better person. So please, on this International Volunteer Day, think about how you can help, and (10) _____ your services.

Word tips

twofold   having two equally important parts
overseas   to or in a foreign country
worldwide   everywhere in the world

Cultural notes

VSO: Voluntary Services Overseas, an international development charity. Founded in 1958, it recruits professionals to work as volunteers, living and working alongside local populations in developing countries, with a vision for a "world without poverty" and a mission to "bring people together to fight poverty".

Peace Corps: A volunteer program run by the United States government. Its stated mission includes providing technical assistance, helping people outside the United States to understand American culture, and helping Americans to understand the cultures of other countries. The work is generally related to social and economic development.

Muslim Aid: A UK based Islamic charity NGO. It currently is run by former senior staff of the Muslim Council of Britain.

Do you know what volunteer is?

Voluntary work includes activities or responsibilities that you take on without obligation or payment. Volunteers contribute time and experience to non-profit organizations and charities for both altruistic（利他的）and self-serving purposes.

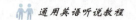

10.1.3 Volunteering helps you live longer

Word tips

journal	a magazine containing articles relating to a particular profession
boost	help something improve
longevity	the fact of having a long life or existence
review	to examine or study again
academic	relating to education, especially education in colleges and universities
well-being	the state of being happy, healthy, or prosperous
associate	to form a connection in your mind between different people or things

1. Before listening to the passage, match the expressions on the left with the ones on the right.

(1)	volunteering can make you happier and	A.	on our health
(2)	doing good	B.	to volunteer
(3)	the effects of volunteerism	C.	a hand
(4)	Australians lead the	D.	review
(5)	36% of the population lending	E.	help you live longer
(6)	systematic	F.	cultural factors
(7)	associated with improvements	G.	deeds for others
(8)	biological and	H.	sense of happiness
(9)	associated with a willingness	I.	in mental health
(10)	it gives us a deep	J.	way in volunteering

158

2. Listen to the passage and decide whether the following statements are true (T) or false (F).

（1）A new study says volunteering increases your longevity by 22 years.　　　　T / F
（2）Researchers looked at over 400 different studies into volunteering.　　　　T / F
（3）Volunteering reduces the chances of dying in the next seven years.　　　　T / F
（4）Australians seem to be the most willing volunteers.　　　　T / F
（5）A researcher said her work with volunteering was finished.　　　　T / F
（6）The researcher said biological factors create a willingness to volunteer.　　　　T / F
（7）A different study gave three possible reasons why people volunteer.　　　　T / F
（8）The second reason was that volunteering helps reduce stress.　　　　T / F

3. Listen to the passage again and choose the best answer based on what you hear.

（1）Where was the research made available to the public?
A. Online.
B. At a conference.
C. In a newspaper.
D. In a journal.

（2）What do volunteers suffer less from?
A. Poverty.
B. Cholesterol.
C. Depression.
D. Obesity.

(3) What is the percentage of Australian volunteers?
   A. 33.
   B. 34.
   C. 35.
   D. 36.

(4) Why does a researcher think more work is needed?
   A. We need to volunteer more.
   B. A researcher's work is never finished.
   C. To prove volunteering is good for our mental health.
   D. Work is good for us.

(5) What are biological and cultural factors often associated with?
   A. Better health and survival.
   B. Money.
   C. Social resources.
   D. Volunteering.

(6) What did University of Michigan researchers suggest?
   A. A nationwide volunteer programme.
   B. More research.
   C. Three reasons why volunteering is good for us.
   D. Living longer.

(7) What do social connections help to do?
   A. To use up our time.
   B. To reduce stress.
   C. To keep us busy.
   D. To help poor people.

(8) What was the third reason?
   A. Volunteering makes us happy.
   B. We need volunteers.
   C. Volunteering is necessary.
   D. It involves physical activities.

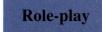 Module 10 Volunteer

| Role-play | Work in groups of four. Each of you will play one of the roles listed below. Read your card carefully and prepare for 3 minutes before you talk in your group. |

Role A   Clean up a river

You think cleaning up a river is the best volunteer project. Tell the others three reasons why. Tell them things that are wrong with their projects. Also, tell the others which is the least useful of these（and why）: Helping out in an animal shelter, lending a hand to restore an important building or planting trees and flowers.

Role B   Animal shelter

You think helping out in an animal shelter is the best volunteer project. Tell the others three reasons why. Tell them things that are wrong with their projects. Also, tell the others which is the least useful of these（and why）: Cleaning up a river, lending a hand to restore an important building or planting trees and flowers.

Role C   Restoring a building

You think lending a hand to restore an important building is the best volunteer project. Tell the others three reasons why. Tell them things that are wrong with their projects. Also, tell the others which is the least useful of these（and why）: Helping out in an animal shelter, cleaning up a river or planting trees and flowers.

Role D   Plant trees and flowers

You think planting trees and flowers is the best volunteer project. Tell the others three reasons why. Tell them things that are wrong with their projects. Also, tell the others which is the least useful of these（and why）: Helping out in an animal shelter, lending a hand to restore an important building or cleaning up a river.

10.1.4 What are the best reasons to volunteer?

1. Listen to the passage and fill in the blanks with what you hear.

Word tips

hone	to make the blade of a knife sharp by rubbing it on a special stone
avenue	one of the methods one can use to achieve something
credit	a source of honor
do one's part	to play one's proper role
make your mark	to achieve success or fame

With so many people volunteering in so many different ways, the (1) _____ reasons for volunteering are almost endless. Probably the best reason of all is to help others by making a difference and giving back to their (2) _____. But what are some of the other best reasons to volunteer?

One of the best reasons to volunteer is that it is tied to something you're (3) _____ about. Maybe you lost a loved one to a disease and want to keep others from suffering the same fate. Maybe you've always loved animals, but your small apartment isn't an ideal home for a large dog, much less two or three. Maybe art has allowed you to express yourself, and you want to share that with others. Volunteering through different programs lets you be (4) _____ to a cause that's close to your heart while spreading that passion to others.

Another great reason to volunteer is that volunteerism can benefit a professional (5) _____. Many employers and schools look favorably upon volunteer experience. Also, while you're volunteering, you can learn new skills and (6) _____ old ones, **honing** your communication, (7) _____, teamwork and time management talents. You'll also have the chance to network with others and possibly vet out a new (8) _____ **avenue**. You might even earn **credits** toward your schooling.

Meeting people and having fun are also good reasons to volunteer. Perhaps you're (9) _____ with plenty of free time on your hands, maybe you have the summer off, or you just have some extra time in the afternoons or on weekends. No matter what your (10) _____ _____, volunteering can keep you busy. You'll be able to meet new people and have exciting experiences, instead of sitting around being bored with little or nothing to do.

Whether you want to **do your part** or **make your mark**, there are many great reasons to volunteer. And those that benefit from your help will just be happy you did, no matter the reason.

Useful expressions

Volunteering provides an opportunity to:
- help the environment
- help others less fortunate or without a voice
- make a difference to the lives of others
- gain confidence and self-esteem
- feel valued and part of a team
- spend quality time away from work or a busy lifestyle
- give something back to an organization that has impacted on one's life, either directly or indirectly

Volunteering can be a route to employment, or a chance of a career change by:
- learning/gaining new skills, knowledge, experiences and sharpening/developing old ones
- honing your communication, leadership, teamwork and time management talents
- networking with others
- gaining an accreditation（认可）
- using one's professional skills and knowledge to benefit others（usually described as pro bono）

Volunteering appeals because of its social benefits such as:
- meeting new people and have exciting experiences
- a chance to socialize
- getting to know the local community

Pair work

2. Read the useful expressions above and discuss what might be other reasons why people are engaged in volunteering. Then write down three most important reasons.

_____
_____
_____

10.1.5 Types of volunteer organizations

> **Word tips**
>
> | | |
> |---|---|
> | non-profit | (of an organization) without the aim of making a profit |
> | -based | (in compounds) containing sth as an important part or feature |
> | category | a group of people or things that have similar qualities |
> | candidate | one of the people competing in an election |
> | recruit | to find new people to work in a company, join an organization, do a job, etc. |
> | dedicated | spending all your time and effort on something |
> | canvass | to try to persuade people to support a political party, politician, plan, etc. by going to see them and talking to them, especially when you want them to vote for you in an election |
> | abound | to exist in very large numbers |
> | expertise | expert knowledge or skill in a particular subject, activity or job |
> | biblical | connected with the Bible; in the Bible |
> | mission | important work |
> | mandate | the authority given to a country to rule another country or region |
> | conservation | the protection of the natural environment |

🔊 **1. Listen to the talk and complete the table.**

Type	Services offered
Political	You may be (1) _____ to **canvass** neighborhoods, help organize voters, organize (2) _____, work the phone banks and help the political process in other ways.
Non-profits	Volunteers step up to provide services to animals, children, students, the sick, the (3) _____ and others who need help on a (4) _____ or long-term basis.
Faith-based	The **mission** is to reach out to the local, national and/or (5) _____ community and (6) _____ the **mandate** of helping those less fortunate. Disaster (7) _____, feeding the hungry, assisting in medical (8) _____, and working within the local community are all opportunities to volunteer.
International	Some organizations, such as the Peace Corps, need volunteers who are willing to travel, while nearly all organizations need willing workers who can help raise (9) _____ to support a variety of (10) _____ areas, such as **conservation**, disaster relief, education, food, health and water resources.

10.1.6 Where to volunteer your time

> **Word tips**
>
> pantry — a very small room in a house where food is kept
> copyedit — to correct and prepare (a manuscript, for example) for typesetting and printing
> patron — someone who supports the activities of an organization, for example by giving money
> flyer — a small sheet of paper that advertises a product or an event and is given to a large number of people
> intermediate — being or occurring at the middle place, stage, or degree or between extremes

🔊 **Listen to the talk. Write in the missing words.**

If you have got the drive to volunteer, check out these 3 non-profits for excellent volunteer opportunities that require no (1) _____ experience.

- **Food pantries**

Food pantries and soup kitchens can always use a helping hand organizing a local food drive, raising money, or simply handing out hot meals to those in need. Offer any specific skills you may have, such as **copyediting**, data (2) _____, or even cooking, and you can be of great value to these organizations.

- **Local libraries**

When I was a (3) _____, I volunteered at my **local library** for a few hours a week for a school project. I liked it so much that I ended up volunteering every week and developed a life-long love of books, as well as an (4) _____ for learning and reading. Libraries typically need help organizing (5) _____ and assisting **patrons**, and you may also be of help setting up and running public events, such as author signings and book fairs. Ask your local library if you can help design **flyers** or copyedit ads, and put that experience on your resume.

- **Retirement homes**

Retirees love an exciting new lecture to (6) _____ or class to teach them something fun and interesting, so be (7) _____ and develop a program that shows off your skills. Are you good at public speaking, or do you want to get better at it? Ask to recite some famous (8) _____ speeches, or to moderate a (9) _____ reading. If you're good with computers, lend your services and teach senior citizens how to perform basic or **intermediate** computer tasks. Chances are that they want to learn, but no one has ever taken the time to give them the proper (10) _____.

10.2 Critical thinking and speaking

Task 1

You are going to read a passage with ten statements attached to it. Each statement contains information given in one step. Identify the step from which the information is derived.

How to volunteer: 10 steps to follow

Volunteering is a great way to further a cause, support an organization, and make a difference in your community. It can also be an opportunity to meet new people and learn new skills. If you'd like to give something besides money, consider lending your time and talents to organizations that are important to you. It is an opportunity to serve.

1. Consider why you want to volunteer. Do you want to help the world or your community? Do you want to build your own skills, make new friends, and learn? Do you love what you do? Do you want to share your gifts with others or give something back? Examining these sorts of questions can help you choose the right direction for your volunteer work.

2. Choose an organization that is meaningful to you. If you feel strongly about literacy, for instance, volunteer at your local library or find out if there is an organization of volunteer tutors in your area. There are organizations doing all sorts of work, and it is especially important with volunteer work that you choose something that you value.

3. Look for an organization or activity in your area or community. While some volunteers do sign up for the Peace Corps or other worldwide organizations and travel to remote parts of the world, you should probably start on a smaller scale than that, especially if you already have commitments at home. If you do plan on venturing abroad in your volunteer work, get lots of information about what to expect there. Talk to others who have traveled with your intended organization and ask them to share their experiences, too.

4. Seek out an organization and tasks within it that suit your skills and interests. If you're an outgoing "people person", you might not have much fun in the back office stuffing envelopes or filing papers. Others, by contrast, might find it uncomfortable to solicit funds door-to-door. Do you love to work with people? With animals? Are you handy? Do you love to speak or to write? Organizations need all sorts of skills. If you're not sure what sort of work you like or dislike, a volunteer organization may be a great opportunity to dabble a bit and try different things.

5. Start small. If you already have a busy schedule, volunteer your time for an hour or two per week or perhaps one day per month. (Just about anybody can free up that much time easily. Try turning off the TV!) You might be surprised how much you can accomplish in even a little bit of time. Then, if you find you enjoy the work and have more time to pursue it, gradually take on more.

6. Get to know others in the organization and how the group supports volunteers. Attend a training or orientation session, if one is available; if not, talk to local group leaders and other volunteers in the community about their experiences. You'll learn what to expect of an organization and your work with it, and you'll pick up some good tips to make your work there more productive and more meaningful.

7. Explain your own background and preferences to those in charge. They can help to match you with meaningful, suitable tasks, but only if they know a bit about who you are. Ask, don't demand. The people in charge of organizing, whether or not they are also volunteers, have certain needs to meet and may be quite busy. Especially if you're just starting out, consider helping with an immediate need even if it is not the ideal match for your abilities.

8. Get started. Ask plenty of questions and do your research, but until you sign up and get your feet wet, you won't know if volunteering for a particular organization is really right for you.

9. Get training. If your organization has a formal orientation or training, attend it. If not, or if you still don't know where to begin, ask to work with an experienced volunteer or group. Then, ask lots of questions and give it a shot.

10. Try not to give up. Volunteer organizations, too, sometimes have less-pleasant tasks, difficult fellow workers, busy times, slow times, or bad management. If you find your work unpleasant, you have choices:
- Get help. If you're overwhelmed, confused, or stuck, ask if there is anyone else that could step up and give you a hand.
- Fix the problem. Lead the charge to get more volunteers, more money, better equipment, or skilled help. Suggest （gently, please!） how matters could be better handled or organized.
- Take a break or back off. If you're exhausted, you may not be doing yourself or anyone else any good. Would everybody be better off if you came back with fresh energy later?

Step	What to do
1	• If you find your work unpleasant, ask if there is anyone else that could step up and give you a hand.
2	• Examining some detailed questions can help you choose the right direction for your volunteer work.
3	• Try to volunteer for an hour or two per week or perhaps one day per month if you have a busy schedule.
4	• Should your organization offers a formal orientation or training, attend it. If not, ask to work with an experienced volunteer or group.
5	• If you have commitments at home, you may as well start an organization in your area or community.
6	• Ask plenty of questions and do your research, and then get started.
7	• You'll learn what to expect of an organization and your work if you know others in the organization and how the group supports volunteers.
8	• Look for a meaningful work or organization for yourself.
9	• If they know a little more about who you are, they can help match you with meaningful suitable tasks.
10	• You'd better find an organization and tasks within it that suit your skills and interests.

Group work

Discuss with group members about the following questions:

（1）Is it necessary to follow all the 10 steps above before you decide where to volunteer? Why or why not?

（2）If not, which steps are far more important than others?

（3）Do you know any volunteer organization from home and abroad? Share your knowledge with each other.

（4）Are you now working for any volunteer organizations? If yes, describe the organization and your work in it to your partners. If not, are you willing to try?

Task 2

Read the short passage and answer the questions.

UNNC students set to spend summer volunteering in rural areas

More than 200 students from the University of Nottingham Ningbo China (UNNC) are set to spend part of their summer holidays volunteering in disadvantaged communities in China and around the world.

The students, who study a wide variety of courses, will take part in two- to three-week volunteering programs teaching in rural areas around China as well as less-developed countries worldwide.

They will travel to provinces in China including Gansu, Henan, Anhui, Guangxi, Guizhou, Yunnan, Jiangsu, Sichuan, Xingjiang and Hunan, as well as to Nepal, Cambodia and Bali. They teach English and other core subjects to primary school students and work on research projects within the local communities.

Organized by student society the Young Volunteers Association (YVA), the volunteering program is an opportunity for students to experience life in economically less-developed areas and countries, and to help make a difference.

The YVA is just one student society on campus that helps hundreds of UNNC students do voluntary work each year.

Nanjie You, Student Activity Support Officer at UNNC, said, "This kind of volunteering is a great opportunity for students to meet and live with people in parts of rural China, and beyond, that are much less developed than many of their home cities. It is a life lesson for many of our Chinese students who were brought up in developed cities such as Beijing, Shanghai or Ningbo."

"This year, more than 20 international students are also taking part in the programs, which will help them make a difference to China and its people, as well as others around the world."

(1) How long will the volunteering programs last?
_____

(2) Which foreign countries and cities will the volunteers travel to?
_____

(3) What services will the volunteering programs offer?
_____

(4) Why does the student society organize these programs?
_____

(5) How many international students participate in the programs?
_____

Assignment

Imagine you are planning to launch a new volunteer organization on campus. You have the experience of being a volunteer tutor for a year. You will work with your partners to work out the following things for your organization:

(1) a proper name;
(2) a logo;
(3) an aim;
(4) services you offer;
(5) how to become a member.

Self-assessment

Review the content covered in this module. How well can you do each of the following?

	very well	well	not well
I know about International Volunteer Day.	○	○	○
I know why volunteer organizations and work are needed.	○	○	○
I know about different types of volunteering activities.	○	○	○
I know where to volunteer my time.	○	○	○

Module 11 Health

We care a lot about our health.
Do you know how to describe your ailment?
Do you know what is superbug?
Do you know what are the top 5 myths about mental health?
Do you know how to read the nutrition facts label?

11.1　Listening and speaking

11.1.1　Describing your ailments

1. Do you know how to describe your aliments? Match the following pictures with the following corresponding expressions.

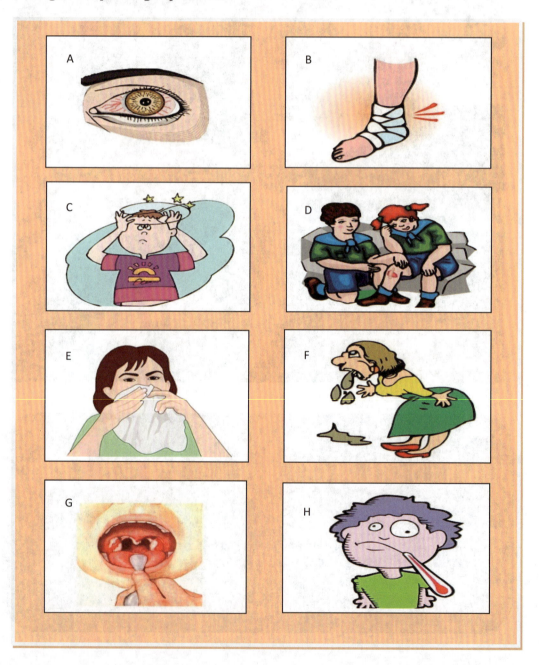

( )	I have a sore throat.
( )	I twist my ankle.
( )	I have a fever.
( )	I have a runny nose.
( )	I feel like throwing up.
( )	I have a pink eye.
( )	I feel dizzy.
( )	I have a cut.

11.1.2 A visit to the doctor's

1. Listen to the dialogue. Write in the missing words.

A: Hi. Come on in and have a seat. Now what seems to be the problem?

B: I have an (1) _____ on my arm.

A: How long have you had (2) _____?

B: It's been about (3) _____.

A: Are you taking anything for it?

B: I (4) _____ but it doesn't seem to be helping.

A: I see. Are you allergic to any medications?

B: Not that I know of.

A: I'm going to give you a prescription for some ointment. I want you to (5) _____.

You should also (6) _____. And it's important to (7) _____.

Make an appointment to see me next week if it doesn't get better over the next few days.

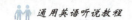

| Role-play | Work in groups of 6（4 patients and 2 doctors）and role-play the following situation. |

Patient A, B, C, D:

You are a patient. Visit your doctor and tell them about your condition. Write down your doctor's recommendations in the table below. You should "get a second opinion". Visit two doctors for each ailment.（See activity card on the next page.）

Doctor's name	Medical condition	Prescription	Prescription directions	Other advice
Dr. Jung	rash	ointment	apply three times a day	Avoid scratching skin. Don't use soap.

Warnings: The advice given by the doctors should not be taken as medical advice. The purpose of this sheet is to help students who are studying English as a second language become familiar with expressions they might hear or need when visiting a doctor.

Ailment Role Cards

Patient A
Ailment: You have a rash on your arms and legs.
Duration: You have had it for about four days.
Previous medication: You have put some cream on it.

Patient B
Ailment: You have the flu.
Duration: Two days.
Previous medication: You took some aspirin.

Patient C
Ailment: You twisted your ankle.
Duration: You twisted this morning.
Previous medication: You took a painkiller.

Patient D
Ailment: You have a sore throat.
Duration: You have had it for two days.
Previous medication: You have been taking some throat lozenges（throat candies）.

Doctor:
You are a doctor and patients are going to come into your office. Ask them about their condition, prescribe some medicine, and give them some advice.（See activity card on the next page.）

Name	Medical condition	Duration	Prior medication	Allergic to medication? Y/N
Mary	rash	1 week	cream	No

Warnings: The advice given by doctors here should not be taken as medical advice. The purpose of this sheet is to help students who are studying English as a second language become familiar with expressions they might hear or need when visiting a doctor.

Doctor Treatment List

Ailment: flu
Prescribe: antiviral medication
　　　　　　Take three times daily after meals.
Extra advice: （1）Get lots of rest.
　　　　　　　（2）Drink plenty of fluids.

Ailment: sore throat
Prescribe: some medication
　　　　　　Take every four hours.
Extra advice: （1）Drink plenty of liquids.
　　　　　　　（2）Drink warm tea with honey.

Ailment: rash
Prescribe: an ointment
　　　　　　Apply four times a day.
Extra advice: （1）Avoid scratching your skin.
　　　　　　　（2）Use as little soap as possible.

Ailment: twisted ankle
Prescribe: some painkillers
　　　　　　Take whenever you have pain （maximum five times daily）.
Extra advice: （1）Keep your foot elevated.
　　　　　　　（2）Keep ice on it for 15 minutes.

11.1.3 Top 5 myths about mental health

🔊 1. Listen to the passage. Write in the missing words.

After years of working online with thousands of people writing to us, we have gathered together what we consider to be the top 5 most common myths about mental health problems. We feel that by getting the word out about these myths, we might help reduce the misunderstandings about mental disorders which seem to be so prevalent in our society today.

(1) _____

In fact, nearly 1 out of every 5 Americans will have a diagnosable mental disorder within their lifetimes, according to the National Institute of Mental Health.

(2) _____

Mental health problems are not caused by solely bad genes or a biological chemical imbalance, according to the research we have to date. Any health care professional, doctor, or mental health advocate who claims otherwise is telling you a half-truth to forward their own, unspoken agendas.

(3) _____

So many times, individuals with a newly diagnosed disorder such as depression or anxiety are told they have to take medication for it. Yet, when they question their physician about how long they must remain on the medication, they receive a mushy, non-answer, such as, "As long as you need to." Most medications prescribed for mental disorders should be taken for short-term symptom relief.

(4) _____

The first part of this statement may not be so much a myth, as most people who have a mental health problem do not seek treatment for it. Rather, they rely on their traditional coping mechanisms (such as exercise, eating, hanging out with friends, working longer and harder, etc.) to take care of the problem. Many problems which may be diagnosable may also be mild enough for this type of care to be sufficient. Talking with friends, reading a self-help book on the subject, or visiting an online self-help support group may be enough to get you through it.

(5) _____

Suicidal feelings are most often symptoms of depression or a related mood disorder. Feeling suicidal does not make you any more or less crazy than anybody else. Suicidal feelings go away once you begin to receive adequate care for your depression or other mood disorder. That's why it is so tragic when people actually succeed in taking their own lives ... Had the person been receiving adequate treatment, they could be alive and feeling much less depressed and suicidal.

11.1.4 Superbugs

1. Listen to the passage. Write in the missing words.

There are many horror movies about superbugs that (1) _____ around the world and kill millions of people. The World Health Organization (WHO) has said the spread of (2) _____ superbugs is now a reality. Many of the medicines that we have used for decades to keep away disease no (3) _____ work. Bugs have developed and have become (4) _____ to antibiotics and other drugs. The WHO said this is a(n) (5) _____ threat to our health. The organization said nobody on Earth is safe. The superbugs can kill healthy people in rich countries as (6) _____ as weaker people in poorer nations. The WHO looked at (7) _____ from 114 countries. It found that some antibiotics that worked 30 years ago do not work now for about (8) _____ the people who take them.

The WHO's (9) _____ director-general for health security Keiji Fukuda describes a(n) (10) _____ future. He said, "The world is headed for a post-antibiotic (11) _____, in which common infections and minor injuries which have been treatable for (12) _____ can once again kill." This means that soon there will be no way to stop people from once again (13) _____ from diseases like malaria, tuberculosis, and influenza. Dr. Fukuda warned this was a global (14) _____. He said, "This is not a regional phenomenon. This is not a phenomena occurring in (15) _____ poor countries or developing countries, or in rich countries or developed countries. This is something which is (16) _____ _____ in all countries in the world."

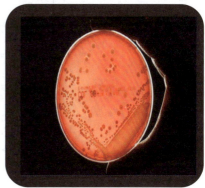

Group discussion

2. Questions for discussion.

- Why haven't scientists made new medicines for superbugs?
- Are you worried about this?
- What should governments do about this?
- What superbugs and viruses do you know about?

11.2 Critical thinking and speaking

Task 1

Nutrition facts label

1. The following is a standard nutrition facts label. Try to describe this label by using the given information.

```
Nutrition Facts
Serving Size 2/3 cup (55g)
Servings Per Container About 8

Amount Per Serving
Calories 230          Calories from Fat 40
                                    % Daily Value*
Total Fat 8g                              12%
   Saturated Fat 1g                        5%
   Trans Fat 0g
Cholesterol 0mg                            0%
Sodium 160mg                               7%
Total Carbohydrate 37g                    12%
   Dietary Fiber 4g                       16%
   Sugars 1g
Protein 3g

Vitamin A                                 10%
Vitamin C                                  8%
Calcium                                   20%
Iron                                      45%

* Percent Daily Values are based on a 2,000 calorie diet.
  Your daily value may be higher or lower depending on
  your calorie needs.
                    Calories:   2,000        2,500
Total Fat          Less than    65g          80g
   Sat Fat         Less than    20g          25g
Cholesterol        Less than    300mg        300mg
Sodium             Less than    2,400mg      2,400mg
Total Carbohydrate              300g         375g
   Dietary Fiber                25g          30g
```

Module 11　Health

Notes: The information in the main or top section can vary with each food product; it contains product-specific information. The bottom part contains a footnote with daily values（DVs）for 2,000 and 2,500 calorie diets. This footnote provides recommended dietary information for important nutrients, including fats, sodium and fiber. The footnote is found only on larger packages and does not change from product to product.

Group discussion

2. Here are three nutrition facts labels of chocolate, grains and yogurt. Please describe the nutrition facts with expressions you learned. Then discuss which is good to our health.

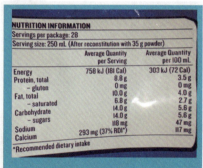

Additional tips

（1）General guide to calories
- 40 calories is low
- 100 calories is moderate
- 400 calories or more is high

（2）Health experts recommend that you keep your intake of saturated fat, trans fat and cholesterol as low as possible as part of a nutritionally balanced diet.

3. Below are two kinds of milk—one is "Reduced Fat Milk", the other is "Non-fat Milk". Each serving size is one cup. Compare two labels and find out which has more calories and more saturated fat, and which one has more calcium.

REDUCED FAT MILK – 2%   NON-FAT MILK

Useful expressions

Comparing and contrasting

- Similar to A, B …
- Likewise …
- Compared with A, B …
- In contrast …
- Different from A, B …
- On the contrary …

Task 2

Health and fitness

Two very fat men enter an ice cream shop. They sit down and order two giant sundaes. After enjoying their rich desserts, they go to a health club and have a good workout. They're trying to work off all those calories they ate. Who would be so silly? Some Americans would. When it comes to health and fitness, Americans have mixed emotions. On the one hand, they are concerned about their health. On the other hand, they have some very unhealthy habits.

Americans know the benefits of having a healthy diet. In school, children learn to eat a variety of healthy foods. People grow up aware of the value of counting calories. They hear about the health dangers of chemicals added to packaged food. They realize they shouldn't eat too many sweets or fats. Many American consumers read labels carefully for nutrition information. That way they can compare products and eat the best foods.

Keeping fit — or maybe getting in shape — is often high on the list of New Year's resolutions for Americans. In the past two decades, fitness has become a fad. Many Americans have joined health clubs to work out with professional equipment. Sports stores sell athletic shoes and clothing for every possible exercise situation. People can even buy weights and equipment and set up their own exercise center at home!

Statistics give health experts good reason to be disappointed. Americans exercise less than they used to. The number of people taking part in fitness activities dropped from 41.7 million in 1991 to only 32 million in 1993. Among high school students, only 37 percent exercise three times per week. However, 70 percent of teenagers watch at least an hour of TV every day, and 38 percent watch over three hours. As a result, the average American gained eight pounds during the 1980's. At least one-third of Americans weigh 20 percent more than their ideal weight.

Still, by many standards, Americans enjoy good health. Medical care in the United States, while expensive, is among the best in the world. The U.S. Government requires strict food inspections to ensure that food is of the highest quality. Food producers must label products accurately. Many resources, such as magazines, TV programs and even the Internet, allow people to find out how to improve their health. Americans know how to make themselves healthier. They just need to do it.

Group discussion

(1) Do you have some bad habits which will influence your health?
(2) What kind of exercises do you usually do to keep fit?

Assignment

Work in pairs and rank these ailments with your partner. Put the one you'd most like a cure for at the top.

Role A   The common cold

You think a cure for the common cold is the most important cure to find. Tell the others three reasons why. Tell them things that aren't as important with their problems. Also, tell the others which is the least important of these to be cured（and why）:stress, overweight or tiredness.

Role B   Stress

You think a cure for stress is the most important cure to find. Tell the others three reasons why. Tell them things that aren't as important with their problems. Also, tell the others which is the least important of these to be cured（and why）:the common cold, overweight or tiredness.

Role C   Overweight

You think a cure for overweight is the most important cure to find. Tell the others three reasons why. Tell them things that aren't as important with their problems. Also, tell the others which is the least important of these to be cured（and why）:the common cold, stress, or tiredness.

Role D   Tiredness

You think a cure for tiredness is the most important cure to find. Tell the others three reasons why. Tell them things that aren't as important with their problems. Also, tell the others which is the least important of these to be cured（and why）:the common cold, stress, or overweight.

Self-assessment

Review the content covered in this module. How well can you do each of the following?

	very well	well	not well
I know how to describe my ailment.	○	○	○
I know what superbugs are.	○	○	○
I know the top 5 myths about mental health.	○	○	○
I know how to read the nutrition facts label.	○	○	○

Module 12 REVIEW

resentation skills | *Further listening and speaking* | *Communication bank*

12.1 Presentation skills

12.1.1 Skills to improve presentation

Even the person with the worst stage fright in the world can improve his or her presentation skills. In fact, many amazing presenters are horribly nervous before they begin their big talk. To improve your presentation skills, all you have to do is learn to relax, have confidence in what you have to say, and follow a few tricks to connect with your audience. It takes time and patience to improve your presentation skills, but if you set your mind to it, you'll be wowing audiences and getting your point across effectively in no time.

Stage 1: Planning for success

Do your research. Hit the Internet and library and talk to experts to get a better idea of your subject, until you feel that you can effectively give a presentation on your subject and answer any questions that will arise along the way.

Know your audience. If you want to polish your presentation skills, then you have to give a lot of thoughts to who will be in the audience. If you know you'll be presenting to your fellow classmates, then you have to think about what will intrigue and interest them. If you're presenting your topic to a group of specialists, then you can assume they know the lingo; if you're presenting a complicated topic to a group of eighth graders, however, then you'll have to simplify it so they can follow along.

Make a plan for your time limit. Whatever your time limit is, you should make your presentation so it fits comfortably under the time limit so you don't spend your time talking fast, trying to hit every point; however, you shouldn't make it so much shorter that you're left with a lot of "dead time" at the end. The closer your presentation is to meeting that time limit, the more relaxed you'll be about presenting your material, and the better your presentation skills will be.

Consider using technology. Technology, from using music or a slide projector, can help enhance your points and engage your audience.

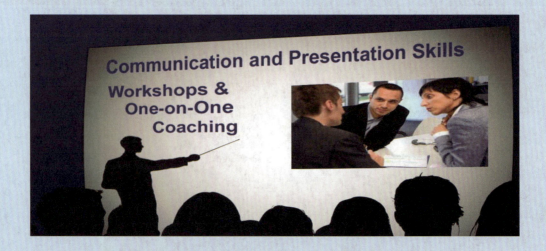

Presentation skills

Using visuals to achieve better effect

Why use visuals?

- to focus the audience's attention
- to illustrate points easier to understand in a visual form but difficult in a verbal form (e.g. statistics)
- to reinforce ideas
- to change focus from aural/oral to visual
- to involve and motivate the audience
- to involve all the senses
- to serve as logical proof
- to save time and avoid putting information on a board
- to avoid turning your back to the audience when writing on a board
- to help the speaker

What are visuals?

- graphs/charts
- maps/photos
- drawings/images
- models videos/films
- objects

What media are used?

- transparencies/slides
- PowerPoint slides
- video projection/projector
- handouts

Stage 2: Presenting with confidence

Drink a tall glass of water to lubricate your vocal chords before you go on stage. Keep a glass or bottle of water with you on stage if it helps you relax and pause occasionally.

Get the audience's attention and signal the beginning.

- Right. Well. OK. Erm. Let's begin.
- Good. Fine. Great. Can we start?
- Shall we start? Let's get the ball rolling.
- Let's get down to business.

Greet audience.

It is important to greet the audience by saying something like:
- Hello, ladies and gentlemen.
- Good morning, members of the jury.
- Good afternoon, esteemed guests.
- Good evening, members of the board.
- Fellow colleagues, Mr. Chairman/Ms. Chairwoman.
- Thank you for your kind introduction.

Introduce oneself (name, position, and company).

Do this not only to give important information so people can identify you but also to establish your authority on the subject and to allow the audience to see your point of view on the subject (you are a student, researcher, responsible for, director of).
- Good afternoon, ladies and gentlemen. Let me introduce myself.
- Good morning, everyone. I'd like to start by introducing myself.
- My name is ...
- I am a student at the INT.
- I am a doctoral candidate.
- I am X. Y. from 3 Com. I'm the manager of ...
- I am a researcher from ... I've been working on the subject now for X years ...

Sometimes, especially when invited to speak, the host introduces the guest, gives the same information as above and then gives the floor to the guest speaker.
- I am very pleased and proud to introduce ... who is ... He/She is known for...
- Now I'll turn the floor over to today's speaker (to take the floor, to have the floor, to give the floor to someone).

Announce your outline.

You want to keep the outline simple so 2 or 3 main points are usually enough.

Concerning grammar, the headings of the outline should be of the same grammatical form.
- I have broken my speech down/up into X parts.
- I have divided my presentation (up) into Y parts.

Embrace the power of "you".

Though you should avoid the second person when you're writing a formal essay, the word "you" is crucial to connecting to your audience during a presentation. You want to make each and every person feel that you're talking to him or her so that the person feels that your presentation can actually benefit him or her. You should say, "You can learn to manage conflict effectively in under an hour with five simple points" instead of "Any person can learn to manage conflict ..."

Repeat your important points.

Though every word in your presentation should count, undoubtedly there will be at least two or three points that you want your audience to walk away with. It's okay to remind your audience of these points by repeating them for emphasis; you can even do so without getting boring or repetitive. If you use a story or anecdote to illustrate a point, remind your audience of what the point is, and return to it later in your presentation, if not at the end. Let your audience see that some of the points you've made are more important than others.

Another way to emphasize your important points is to slow down when you want your audience to really hone in on your words. Use your hands to gesture for emphasis if it's necessary.

Consider making time for a Q & A period.

You should give a time limit for questions, say, 5-10 minutes. Tell your audience that you're going to make this much time for questions so that you don't get off track by answering so many questions that your audience has forgotten the gist of your presentation.

Make sure you have a conclusion after the question period. You don't want to give a stellar presentation and then have it evolve into a series of irrelevant questions.

Finish strong.

Avoid looking bored with your own presentation or eager to get off stage. Don't say something like, "Well, that about covers it" or "That's all I've got". Be confident that you've given a great presentation and be excited about wrapping it up with a nice little bow.

Body language.

Stand at a comfortable distance — Parnell suggests remaining within 2.5-7 feet of your audience. This presupposes (at a subconscious level) a personal to social relationship. Eye contact—Don't surf the audience with your eyes. Rather, make eye contact with one person at a time.

Appear confident:
(a) Shoulders back.
(b) Arms at your sides or held in front of your body when making gestures.
(c) Hands open or only slightly closed.
(d) Smile slightly or keep your face neutral.
(e) Take long stride.
(f) Make every movement purposeful and decided.
(g) Treat props (like your resume or a handout) as though they are of value. Don't let a paper in your hand flap back and forth carelessly.

BODY LANGUAGE SIGNS

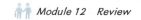

12.1.2 Informative impromptu speech practice

Procedure

Step 1

Explain assignment: You will be given a short 1-minute informative speech.

Informative: Tell the audience about something.

Impromptu: Little to no preparation.

Step 2

Choose a topic from the list.

(1) What is the best way to find a job?

(2) What do you think are the five most common questions asked at a job interview?

(3) What are some things you should do for a job interview? How about things you shouldn't do?

(4) How should a person dress when they go for a job interview?

(5) What are some good things to have on your resume?

(6) What is the best thing to do to stay healthy?

(7) How often do you exercise?

(8) What is your diet like? Do you eat mostly fruits and vegetables?

Step 3

You are given around 5 minutes to prepare your speech. Do not write the speech, but you can jot down notes of key words.

Step 4

Pass out the Peer Evaluation Form. The audience's task is to watch each speech and give an evaluation. Speakers are evaluated on their posture, eye contact, gestures, and voice.

Step 5

Teacher will invite the first student to go to the front of the classroom and give a 1-minute speech.

Step 6

Continue within a group until everyone has had a chance to give a speech.

Step 7

Collect all the evaluations and spread them around the room for everyone to read.

Peer Evaluation Form

Write down the name of each speaker, and take notes under each category.

Name	Posture	Eye contact	Gesture	Voice

12.2 Further listening and speaking

12.2.1 Career search

I. Pre-listening exercises

What jobs are popular among men and women in your country? Are there social or cultural rules that influence what jobs people do?

II. Listening exercises

Listen to the conversation. Match the items on the right to the sentences on the left.

(1) We need to hire a (n) _____ to install a new door in our bedroom.	A. get something
(2) Be patient. It takes some workers to _____ like that.	B. auto mechanic
(3) He is a great _____ because he can repair any vehicle.	C. am suited
(4) The _____ generally don't work if they have saved enough for retirement.	D. carpenter
(5) I don't think I _____ for this kind of of work, so I'm thinking about quitting soon.	E. elderly

III. Post-listening exercises

In the past, what kinds of jobs were mainly done by men or women (a registered nurse, a secretary, or childcare worker)? Is this still true today, or is this trend changing? What are the reasons for these changes: social, religious, or economic?

IV. Online investigations

Use the Internet to find out how the workplace is changing in a different country in terms of men's and women's roles and cultural diversity. Interview a classmate from a different country if possible to understand their views on this topic. Here are some possible questions to consider:

- Are women often more qualified than men to work in positions that were traditionally held by men? If so, what has caused this change?
- Are there any religious principles within certain faiths that influence the degree to which women work outside of the home?
- How do people view men who work in jobs that are often held by more women (nursing, elementary school teachers, secretaries, office clerks, etc.)?

12.2.2 Volunteer work

I. Pre-listening exercises

Have you ever been a volunteer? What famous volunteer groups can you name in your city or country?

II. Listening exercises

Listen to five speakers talking about the values of volunteering. Match the views A-L with speakers 1-5.

Speaker 1 ____ ____	A. Volunteers in general are happier.
	B. Volunteering gives me a sense of self-respect and self-esteem.
Speaker 2 ____ ____	C. It is a real social capital.
	D. Volunteers feel like they have more time, ironically.
	E. It nicely holds us collectively accountable for our community.
Speaker 3 ____ ____	F. It gives me a reason to get out of bed in the morning and be proud of what I did today.
	G. It makes life better for people and makes a better world.
Speaker 4 ____ ____	H. It is a kind of self-satisfaction.

Module 12　Review

	I. It is the way that we can get to know each other.
	J. A research shows that volunteers actually live longer.
Speaker 5 ___ ___	K. It gives me some kind of dignity.
	L. It builds cohesion in our communities.

III. Post-listening exercises

Work in pairs and talk about which one of the following volunteering works you would like to do: Farming in the community, caring children in a day care center, or cleaning a place in the city. Organize your opinion using the form below.

Your choice: _____

First reason: _____

Details: _____

_____

Second reason: _____

Details: _____

_____

199

12.2.3 A healthy lifestyle

I. Pre-listening exercises

Think of five important steps to maintain a healthy lifestyle. Write them down and look up information on the Internet to support these ideas

II. Listening exercises

1. **Listen to the conversation and answer the questions by making choices.**

   (1) What does the man want to do?
   A. He wants to play basketball with friends from work.
   B. He wants to try out for the company baseball team.
   C. He wants to get in shape and compete in a cycling race.

   (2) What is the woman's main concern?
   A. She is worried her husband will spend too much time away from home.
   B. She is afraid her husband will become a fitness freak.
   C. She is concerned about her husband's health.

   (3) What is the woman's first suggestion to her husband?
   A. He should see a doctor.
   B. Her husband should start with a light workout.
   C. Her husband needs to visit a fitness trainer.

   (4) What does the woman advise about the man's diet?
   A. He should consume less salt.
   B. He should eat less fatty foods.
   C. He should add more protein products to his diet.

   (5) Why does the man's wife recommend cycling?
   A. It is good for improving muscle tone.
   B. It helps strengthen the heart.
   C. It helps develop mental toughness.

2. Listen to the conversation again and finish the text.

Man:	Honey, the basketball game is about to (1) _____. And could you bring some (2) _____ and a bowl of ice cream? And ... uh ... a slice of pizza from the fridge.
Woman:	Anything else?
Man:	Nope, that's all for now. Hey, Hon, you know, they're (3) _____ a company basketball team, and I'm thinking about joining. What do you think?
Woman:	Humph ...
Man:	"Humph"? What do you mean by "Humph"? I was the (4) _____ player in high school.
Woman:	Yeah, (5) _____ years ago. Look, I just don't want you having a heart attack (6) _____ up and down the court.

III. Post-listening exercises

Find information on the following topics and discuss your findings with a partner:
- serious health concerns in different countries and solutions to resolving these problems
- a basic daily menu for a healthy lifestyle
- recommended exercises for different age groups and people with certain health risks

IV. Online investigations

There are many companies that promote products promising amazing, and often, unbelievable health claims dealing with anything from weight loss to better memory power. For example, diet plans, weight loss aids and nutritional supplements can provide health benefits, but you have to evaluate claims. So, how can we tell whether the claims are true or not? Search online for a product or service that claims to provide fantastic results, read over the information and identify any parts of the ad that might be deceptive or misleading. Does the ad use an emotional appeal to get you to buy a product? Share your ideas with a partner.

12.3 Communication bank

Talk about job responsibilities
- My main job is to …
- Part of my job involves …
- My responsibilities involve/ include …
- The job description requires me to …
- As … I make sure/ am in charge of /am responsible for …

Talk about benefits/rewards from the job
- The job gives me …
- The job allows me to …
- The best thing about the job is …
- What I enjoy the most about my job is …
- I get to … through the job, which is very important to me.

Agreeing or disagreeing

Agreeing	Disagreeing
I agree.	I disagree.
So do I.	I don't think so.
Me too.	Me neither.
You're right.	I don't either.
That's right.	（No.）That's not right.
Good idea.	Yes, but…
	（I'm sorry, but）I don't agree.

Commenting

- That's interesting. I think that …
- Interesting point. I would add …
- Hmmm. I hadn't thought of that before.
- Can I add something here?
- （Do you）Mind if I interject something here?

Comparing and contrasting

- Similar to A, B …
- Likewise, …
- Compared with A, B …
- In contrast, …
- Different from A, B …

Module 13
Men and Women

"A man's face is his autobiography. A woman's face is her work of fiction."

— Oscar Wilde

"Men marry women with the hope they will never change. Women marry men with the hope they will change. Invariably they are both disappointed."

— Albert Einstein

"Women need to feel loved and men need to feel needed."

— Rita Mae Brown

"A man does what he can; a woman does what a man cannot."

— Isabel Allende

Can you tell any physical or non-physical differences between men and women?
What are your attitudes towards gender equality and gender roles?
What do you think are the top 5 qualities of an ideal husband or wife?

13.1 Listening and speaking

13.1.1 Differences between men and women

Group discussion

1. Do you agree with the differences between men and women described in the following picture? Give your own opinions.

♀		♂
Most often WE start a conversation.	Conversations	And we always end it.
Last man who admitted his mistake was the one who created women.	Admitting	No possibility of women admitting her mistake.
We will give you directions via pubs.	Mistakes	We will give you directions via shops.
We dress up only on three occasions --- seeing the ex-girlfriend, marriage and funeral.	Seeking	Don't need any occasion to dress up. Can dress up and go to the restaurant, to dry cleaner, throw litter, get Xerox copies, and water plants in rain.
All married men are fools. If not, they would have married.	Directions	All married women are wise. If not, they would have remained

Pair work

2. Work in pairs and make a list of other 5 differences between men and women.

（1）	
（2）	
（3）	
（4）	
（5）	

3. Read and judge: Which sex do you think each statement may apply to?
   Note: X=a man/woman, men/women, he/she

Situation	Statement	Men	Women
Bathrooms	The average number of items in a typical American X's bathroom is 437.		√
Going out	When X says he/she is ready to go out, it means X will be ready, as soon as X makes one phone call and finishes putting on the outfit of his/her final decision.		
Eating out	When X gets their check, out come the pocket calculators.		
Groceries	X waits till the only items left in his/her fridge are half a lime and a soda.		
The telephone	X can visit his/her friend for two weeks, and upon returning home, X will call the same friend and they will talk for three hours.		
Dressing up	X will dress up to go shopping, water the plants, empty the garbage, answer the phone, read a book, get the mail.		
Trips	If X goes on a seven-day trip, he/she will pack five days' worth of clothes and will wear some things twice.		
Toys	X never grows out of their obsession with toys.		
Laundry	X will wear every article of clothing X owns before X will do the laundry.		

4. Listen to the passage about interesting differences between men and women and check your judgment in the previous exercise.

5. Listen to the passage and fill in the blanks.

The differences between men and women have spawned (1) _____ , social structures, jokes, psychology streams, (2) _____ approaches and more. Possibly, the entire world is based on the difference between men and women.

Men signify the (3) _____ yang energy in Eastern traditions while women signify the (4) _____ yin energy. Though men and women signify (5) _____ forces in Nature, their complementary nature makes them (6) _____ .

Biologically, both men and women have different body structures, sexual systems and biological (7) _____ . (8) _____ differences between the two have been studied endlessly in psychology streams though the debate continues about the differing (9) _____ levels of men and women. Most people consider men to be of both (10) _____ physical and mental strength as compared to women.

Nature has confined the task of (11) _____ to women alone. This has left the task of nurturing confined to them but the difference is fast becoming (12) _____ with more and more men taking on an "equal partner" role in most relationships.

Women are considered to be weaker at (13) _____ and (14) _____ _____ tasks but are considered better at (15) _____ and (16) _____ _____ tasks. However, these differences are (17) _____ in the modern world with equal opportunities available to both in most cultures, so they are difficult to define.

207

13.1.2 Physical differences between men and women

🔊 1. Listen to a passage about how men and women differ athletically and decide whether the following statements are true（T）or false（F）.

> **Word tips**
>
> skeletal /ˈskelətl/ adj. 骨骼的　　aerobic /eəˈrəʊbɪk/ adj. 有氧的

（1）____ Athletic differences between men and women have much to do with genetics and hormones.
（2）____ Men are more subjected to certain types of athletic injuries than women.
（3）____ Men have more body fat than women.
（4）____ Men's joints are more flexible.
（5）____ Men have larger skeletal muscles as well as larger hearts.
（6）____ Men have a greater aerobic advantage than women.

🔊 2. Do men lose weight faster than women? Listen to the passage and fill in the missing information.

Reasons	Fact: Men do tend to lose weight（1）_____ than women.
Men have more（2）_____.	This allows them to burn more（3）_____.
Women are predisposed to（4）_____ fat.	Women have higher levels of estrogen to make it easier for them to（5）_____.
Men's bodies respond（6）_____ to exercise.	Women's bodies actually go into a sort of（7）_____ mode, slowing the metabolism to hang onto more fat.
Women may have a lower（8）_____ for exercise.	Women have smaller（9）_____ than men, which can make women feel as though they are working（10）_____ than men even if the women are working at the same level.
Conclusion	（11）_____ along with hormones, play a large role in how quickly some people lose weight.

> **Word tips**
>
> predisposed /priːdɪˈspəʊzd/ adj. 使倾向于……的
> estrogen /ˈiːstrədʒən/ n. 雌激素
> metabolism /meˈtæbəlɪzəm/ n. 新陈代谢

Module 13 Men and Women

13.1.3 Non-physical differences between men and women

Pair discussion   1. *Do you agree or disagree? Why?*

（1）Women talk more than men.
（2）Men only speak when there's something important to say.
（3）Men and women love gossip equally.
（4）Men talk more about relationships than women.
（5）Men: Women talk too much!
（6）Women: Men don't talk enough!

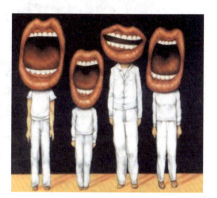

2. Listen to the passage and check your answers to the questions in the previous exercise.

Who speaks more, men or women? Most people wouldn't （1）_____ to say that women speak more. There are many jokes about how much and what women talk about. But research which some may find surprising （2）_____ that both men and women speak more or less （3）_____.

Four hundred university students in the United States and Mexico participated in the study. Researchers recorded the students' daily （4）_____ for several days. After analyzing the data, they discovered that both sexes are in a （5）_____ dead heat（不分上下）when it comes to speaking. Women used a little more than（6）_____ words every day. Men used a little （7）_____ than 16,000 words. The report admits, though, that the numbers could change as men and women grow （8）_____ , because the study only tracked university students.

The current idea that women are （9）_____ just isn't true. In addition, men only speak when they have something （10）_____ to say also isn't true. Both ideas probably come from cultural and political （11）_____ against women. But the study explains that men （12）_____ just as much as women. Men and women also talk equally about （13）_____ topics. But women actually talk more about （14）_____ .

A psychologist at Yale University has a somewhat different opinion. She suggests that the idea about men and women probably come from （15）_____ between the genders. Unfortunately, the study doesn't know how speaking （16）_____ change in an argument. But other studies have supported the （17）_____ that guys become quiet and women talk more in an emotional （18）_____ .

3. Are women really better at learning languages? Listen to a report and choose the best answer to the following questions.

(1) Which statement is NOT true according to the passage?
   A. There are more female students at most British universities.
   B. Generally speaking, females do better in school than males at most British universities.
   C. It is long held true that females are adept at both native tongue and foreign language study.
   D. Sex is the only factor that contributes to an individual's language proficiency.

(2) When processing language, _____.
   A. boys' brains show greater activity in the areas used for language encoding
   B. girls' brains show activity in the areas associated with visual and aural functions
   C. boys can process an abstract piece of language more efficiently
   D. for males, the most effective way to study language is to learn visually as well as orally

(3) In terms of strategy use, _____.
   A. studies concluded that female and male foreign language learners tend to use study methods equally
   B. studies concluded that female foreign language learners tend to use more varied study methods than their male peers
   C. studies concluded that female foreign language learners tend to use less varied study methods than their male peers
   D. females tend to stick with only a handful of study methods

(4) Language learning site *Busuu* has reported that _____.
   A. female users visit their language learning websites more frequently
   B. male users visit their language learning websites more frequently
   C. female users of the site are more likely to converse with native speakers
   D. male users of the site never converse with native speakers

(5) Which statement is true according to the passage?
   A. Girls tend to be more motivated to study languages than their male classmates.
   B. Male students are more likely to continue their foreign language studies in school.
   C. Since language teachers are typically women, boys in the classroom can connect to their instructor as a role model.
   D. Both girls and boys perceive language study as a male domain.

Module 13 Men and Women

13.1.4 Gender equality

1. Match the terms on the left with the definitions on the right.

Terms	Definitions
(1) equal rights	A. increasing the spiritual, political, social or economic strength of women
(2) female headed households	B. the act of excluding women from something
(3) feminism	C. sexual behavior that annoys or upsets someone
(4) gender discrimination	D. the belief or attitude that one gender or sex is inferior to or less valuable than the other
(5) women empowerment	E. having the same rights, treatment, etc. of women
(6) Women's exclusion	F. families taken care of by a woman
(7) sexual harassment	G. the belief that women should be allowed the same rights, power and opportunities as men and be treated in the same way, or the set of activities intended to achieve this state

2. Fill in the blanks with the terms in the previous exercise.

(1) Women in _____ often bear the burden of ensuring household survival.
(2) Girls and boys must have _____ in education.
(3) The university has been accused of _____ because it has so few women professors.
(4) Women's _____ from political, educational and economic opportunities is a hindrance to women _____.
(5) She had a lifelong commitment to _____.
(6) When a man talks dirty to a woman, it's _____.

211

🔊 **3. Listen to the passage about Japanese women to have more equality and decide whether the following statements are true（T）or false（F）.**

_____（1）Japan's civil service will be 50 percent female by 2020.
_____（2）New equality laws aim to prevent the workforce from shrinking more.
_____（3）There are five times more female managers in America than in Japan.
_____（4）One third of Japanese women do not work again after childbirth.
_____（5）Japan's firms want to measure levels of sexual harassment.
_____（6）Female entrepreneurs will learn to drive.
_____（7）Japan's Prime Minister wants to create a gender-equality society.
_____（8）Japan is next to last in a UN index comparing gender equality.

13.2 Critical thinking and speaking

Task 1

Sayings quiz: Men and women

1. The saying "Behind every successful man is a woman" suggests that women often _____.
 A. cost a lot
 B. discourage men
 C. encourage men

2. "Boys will be boys" might be said to justify _____.
 A. children failing exams
 B. men having a fight
 C. boys doing their homework

3. The saying "It's a man's world" implies that life is _____.
 A. neutral
 B. fair
 C. unfair

4. The saying "Women will have the last word" suggests that men stop speaking _____.
 A. before women stop
 B. after women stop
 C. when women stop

5. If "the way to a man's heart is through his stomach", a woman may gain a man's affections with _____.
 A. flattery
 B. money
 C. food

The IRON Lady

"If you want something said, ask a man. If you want something done, ask a woman."
—Margaret Thatcher 1925–2013

Task 2

Gender roles

Read the following passage and cross out（"/"）the inappropriate words according to the context.

（1）**Sex/Gender** refers to **physical or physiological** differences between males and females, including both their primary and secondary sex characteristics. （2）**Sex/Gender**, on the other hand, refers to **social or cultural** distinctions associated with being male or female. Scholars generally regard gender as a social construct — meaning that it does not exist naturally, but is instead a concept that is created by culture and societal norms.

The term **gender role** refers to society's concept of how men and women are expected to act and behave. These roles are based on **norms, or standards** created by society. In American culture, （3）**masculine/feminine** roles are usually associated with strength, aggression, and dominance, while （4）**masculine/feminine** roles are usually associated with passivity, nurturing, and subordination.

Role learning starts with socialization at birth. Even today, our society is quick to outfit （5）**male/female** infants in blue and girls in pink, even applying these color-coded gender labels while a baby is in the womb. **Gender socialization** occurs through **four major agents**（因素）: **family, education, peer groups, and mass media**. Each agent reinforces gender roles by creating and maintaining normative expectations for gender-specific behavior. Exposure also occurs through **secondary agents** such as **religion and the workplace**. Repeated exposure to these agents over time leads men and women into a false sense that they are acting naturally, rather than following a socially constructed role.

Cross-cultural studies reveal that **children** are aware of gender roles by age **two or three**, and at four or five, most children are firmly entrenched（根深蒂固的）in culturally appropriate gender roles. Parents often supply （6）**boys/girls** with trucks, toy guns, and superhero paraphernalia, which are active toys that promote motor skills, aggression, and solitary play. （7）**Daughters/Sons** are often given dolls and dress-up apparel that foster nurturing, social proximity, and role-play. Studies have shown that children will most likely choose to play with "**gender appropriate**" toys even when cross-gender toys are available because parents give children positive feedback（in the form of praise, involvement and physical closeness）for gender normative behavior.

The drive to adhere to masculine or feminine gender roles continues later in life. (8) **Men/Women** tend to outnumber (9) **men/women** in professions such as law enforcement, the military, and politics. (10) **Men/Women** tend to outnumber (11) **men/women** in care-related occupations such as childcare, healthcare, and social work. These **occupational roles** are examples of typical American male and female behavior, derived from the culture's traditions. Adherence to these roles demonstrates **fulfillment of social expectations** but **not necessarily personal preference**.

The attitudes and expectations surrounding gender roles are **not typically based on any inherent or natural gender differences**, but on **gender stereotypes, or oversimplified notions** about the attitudes, traits, or behavior patterns of women or men. Gender stereotypes form the basis of **sexism**, or the prejudiced beliefs that value one sex over another. Sexism varies in its level of severity. In parts of the world where (12) **Men/women** are strongly undervalued, young girls may not be given the same access to nutrition, healthcare, and education as boys. Further, they will grow up believing that they deserve to be treated differently from boys. While illegal in the United States when practiced as **discrimination**, unequal treatment of women continues to pervade social life. It should be noted that discrimination based on sex occurs at both the micro- and macro-levels; discrimination that is built into the social structure is known as institutional discrimination（制度歧视）.

American society allows for some level of **flexibility** when it comes to the acting out of gender roles. To a certain extent, men can assume some feminine roles and women can assume some masculine roles without serious repercussions; however those that step outside of what society deems acceptable face consequences. Gender roles not only **shape individual behavior**, but **penalize those that don't conform to these norms** — especially those that do not identify as male or female. Transgender, genderqueer, and other non-conforming gender people face discrimination, oppression, and violence for not adhering to society's traditional gender roles. People who identify as gay, lesbian, bisexual, or queer are also ostracized for breaking the traditional gender norm of who a person of a given gender "should" be attracted to. Even people who identify as cisgender（identifying with the sex they were assigned at birth）and straight（attracted to the opposite gender）face repercussions if they step outside of their gender role in an obvious way.

☆ *Would you say your country was a male-dominated one?*

☆ *Are there areas in your society where gender inequality hits men?*

☆ *Have you ever felt discrimination?*

Task 3

How acceptable do you think each of the following is?

Pair work — Discuss with your partner about your attitudes toward the following phenomenon. Try to support your opinion with your reflections on the previous reading passage.

Note:
1= definitely acceptable
2= acceptable
3= not sure
4= unacceptable
5= definitely unacceptable

☆ Men crying watching sad movies ☐

☆ Boys playing with Barbie dolls ☐

☆ Men wearing make-up ☐

☆ Male nurses ☐

☆ Househusbands ☐

☆ Women asking men out on dates ☐

☆ Women using bad language ☐

☆ Female fighter plane pilots ☐

☆ Female religious leaders ☐

☆ Female boxing ☐

Task 4

Top 5 qualities women look for in a man

In today's society, young decent men are rare to find. It seems as though manly men are a symbol of the past and now are officially gone. However, decent men still exist. Keep these 5 qualities in mind when looking for Mr. Right, so you don't lose sight of him.

 #1 Strong moral code

A man who abides by a moral code is definitely a keeper. He is the type of man who knows the difference between right and wrong. He always grounds his decisions in life on an understanding of a high moral ground.

 #2 Good relationships with his family

A man who has a close and loving relationship with his family is a man you want to be with. This type of man knows the importance of family and truly cherishes family time. Also, a man who treats his mother with respect will most likely treat you with respect and is obviously worth having as a husband.

 #3 Hard work ethic

A man who has a hard work ethic is marriage material. He will never give up when working towards his ambitions. He will always work hard to provide your future family financial support, no matter what circumstances come his way. He will also instill this same value in your future children.

 # 4 Shared life goals

A man who shares similar life goals with you will make for a great husband. Sharing that similarity with you, he will most likely support your efforts in life. He will always be there to comfort you when you hit your lows and rejoice with you when you achieve your goals.

 # 5 Selfless

A man who puts others before himself and gives a helping hand to those in need is a man you should not overlook. A man who values selflessness will most likely be a loving, supportive husband and father.

Yes, a decent man that you want to share a beautiful marriage with is out there. Although he may not be easy to spot, he will come and sweep you off your feet when you least expect it. Just make sure that he has these qualities, so you know you two

Assignment

Group presentation

What are the top 5 qualities men look for in a woman?

Work in groups and prepare a 5-minute-long presentation on the top 5 qualities men look for in a woman for a marriage. You may follow the format used in the preceding passage.

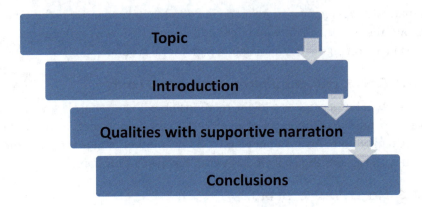

- Topic
- Introduction
- Qualities with supportive narration
- Conclusions

Module 13　Men and Women

Self-assessment

Review the content covered in this module. How well can you do each of the following?

	very well	well	not well
I can describe some differences between men and women.	○	○	○
I can express my own attitudes towards gender equality and gender roles.	○	○	○
I have some insights into the top qualities either sex is looking for in the opposite.	○	○	○
I can deliver a mini speech by following the traditional format introduced in the passage.	○	○	○

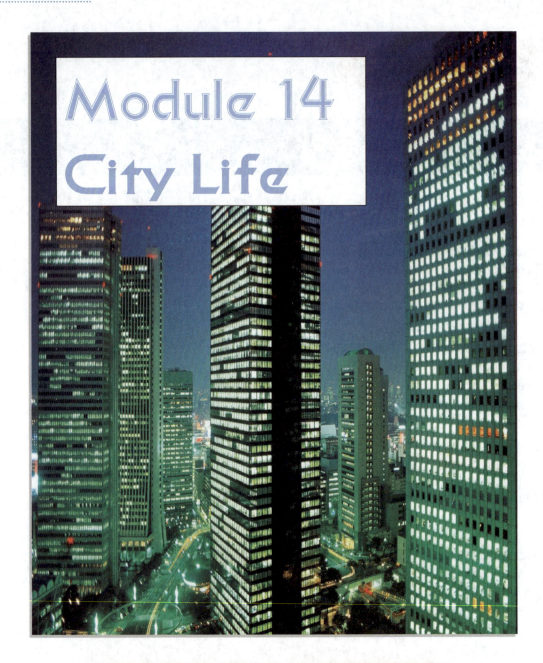

Module 14
City Life

Do you live in cities? Do you like city life?
In this module, your will:
- learn to compare life in cities and life in the country.
- learn to describe different urban lifestyle choices.
- learn about some negative influence or facts of city life.
- learn about the pace of life in cities.

Module 14 City Life

14.1 Listening and speaking

14.1.1 The city and the country

🔊 1. Listen to the dialogue. Choose the correct answer to these statements based on the dialogue.

(1) Carol thinks life in the city is more interesting than that in the country.

☐ True
☐ False

(2) Steven says that the city is less dangerous than the country.

☐ True
☐ False

(3) The people in the countryside aren't as open as those in the city.

☐ True
☐ False

(4) The country is quieter than the city.

☐ True
☐ False

(5) Living in the city isn't as expensive as that in the country.

☐ True
☐ False

(6) Life in the country is healthier than that in the city.

☐ True
☐ False

(7) Carol thinks the city is more fun than the country.

☐ True
☐ False

(8) Steven thinks Carol is crazy for leaving the country.

☐ True
☐ False

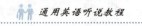

(9) Carol says she might move back to the country when she is married and has children.

☐ True
☐ False

(10) Life in the country isn't as hectic as life in the city.

☐ True
☐ False

🔊 **2. Listen to the dialogue again and write in the missing information.**

Steven:	How do you like living in the big city?
Carol:	There are many things that are better than living in the country!
Steven:	Can you give me some examples?
Carol:	Well, it certainly is (1) _____ than the country. There is so much more to do and see!
Steven:	Yes, but the city is (2) _____ than the country.
Carol:	That's true. People in the city are (3) _____ those in the countryside.
Steven:	I'm sure that the country is (4) _____, too!
Carol:	Yes, the city is busier than the country. However, the country is (5) _____ than the city.
Steven:	I think that's a good thing!
Carol:	Oh, I don't. The country is so slow and boring! It's (6) _____ than the city.
Steven:	How about the cost of living? Is the country cheaper than the city?
Carol:	Oh, yes. The city is (7) _____ than the country.
Steven:	Life in the country is also (8) _____ than in the city.
Carol:	Yes, it's (9) _____ in the country. But, the city is so much more exciting. It's (10) _____ than the country.
Steven:	I think you are crazy for moving to the city.
Carol:	Well, I'm young now. Maybe when I'm married and have children I'll move back to the country.

Module 14 City Life

Pair work

When comparing the city with the country in a conversation, you'll need to use the *comparative form*. Practice comparing the city with the country with the above dialogue and then practice your own conversations with your partner by using comparative form.

14.1.2 A super city—good or bad?

🔊 **1. Listen to the passage and fill in the blanks with the numbers you hear.**

(1) The Local Government Commission today recommended that the ____ councils in the Wellington region become ____, called the Greater Wellington Council.

(2) There would be ____ mayor and ____ councillors.

(3) The change would happen at the time of the local body elections in _____.

(4) People have the chance to give their written feedback by _____.

(5) The _____ Wairarapa councils do not want to be part of a Wellington super city.

🔊 **2. Listen to the passage again and answer the following questions.**

(1) What is each smaller region responsible for?
_____.

(2) What are the concerns of some people for a super city?
_____.

(3) What is the benefit of a super city to some small councils according to other people?
_____.

(4) In the eyes of many Kapiti residents, what are the advantages of being part of Wellington?
_____.

14.1.3 Urban lifestyle choice

Do you want to live in a busy area or a quiet area?

Would you prefer a lot of appliances or antiques?

Do you want to move in to a furnished apartment or an unfurnished apartment?

Do you want to have a small yard or a big yard?

Do you want to live near a train station or a park?

Interview a partner about their lifestyle choices and then write a short report.

For example:

"I interviewed Monica and she told me she wanted to live in a busy area because she likes to go to markets and see all the different activities. She also wants a lot of appliances in her house because they make her life easier ..."

_____
_____
_____
_____
_____
_____

14.1.4 City living makes it harder to concentrate

🔊 **1. Listen to the talk and decide whether these statements are true（T） or false（F）.**

（1）	A new report says it's difficult for people to study in cities.	T / F
（2）	People who live in the countryside can focus better than city people.	T / F
（3）	The research team studied a tribe in South Africa.	T / F
（4）	The team studied two different tribes from the town and the country.	T / F
（5）	The research might change how companies work in the future.	T / F
（6）	The researcher said many things around us help us think better.	T / F
（7）	Billions have relocated to urban areas in the past 100 years.	T / F
（8）	Many people originally from the countryside might return.	T / F

🔊 **2. Listen to the talk again and write in the missing words.**

A new report says living in a city makes it （1）_____ for people to concentrate. The research found that people who live in rural areas can （2）_____ better than people in urban areas. The study is from Goldsmiths College, which is （3）_____ of the University of London. Head researcher Dr. Karina Linnell and her team studied how two groups of people did the same "thinking （4）_____". The team went to a （5）_____ _____ part of Namibia, southwest Africa, to study the Himba tribe. Himba people live a very (6) _____ life in the desert, doing (7) _____ farming. The team also studied members of the same tribe who had moved to the (8) _____ town. Dr. Linnell said the tribe who lived in the desert did much better on the tests than those in the town.

Dr. Linnell's research may change the way companies (9) _____. In the future, workers may (10) _____ from cities to live and work in the countryside. Linnell said there are too many things around us in the city that (11) _____ us from thinking about one thing for a long time. This means we do not work at our (12) _____. She asked, "What if, for example, companies realized (13) _____ tasks would be better carried out by employees (14) _____ outside of the urban environment where their concentration ability is better?" The past century has seen (15) _____ of people move from the countryside to big cities. If Dr. Linnell's research is true, this (16) ___ _____ might see many of those people return to the great outdoors.

14.1.5 Traffic in cities

🔊 *Listen to the talk and write in the missing words.*

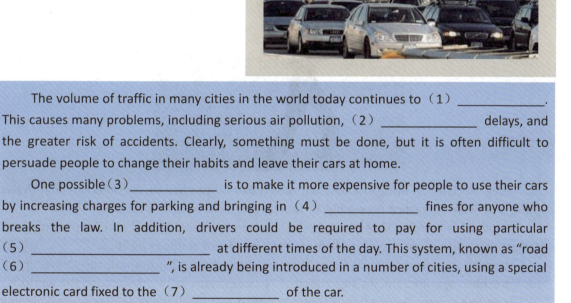

The volume of traffic in many cities in the world today continues to (1) _____. This causes many problems, including serious air pollution, (2) _____ delays, and the greater risk of accidents. Clearly, something must be done, but it is often difficult to persuade people to change their habits and leave their cars at home.

One possible (3) _____ is to make it more expensive for people to use their cars by increasing charges for parking and bringing in (4) _____ fines for anyone who breaks the law. In addition, drivers could be required to pay for using particular (5) _____ at different times of the day. This system, known as "road (6) _____", is already being introduced in a number of cities, using a special electronic card fixed to the (7) _____ of the car.

Another way of dealing with the problem is to provide cheap parking on the (8) _____ of the city, and strictly control the number of (9) _____ allowed into the centre. Drivers and their passengers then use a special bus service for the final stage of their journey.

Of course, the most important thing is to provide good public transport. However, to get people to give up the comfort of their cars, public transport must be felt to be reliable, convenient and comfortable, with (10) _____ kept at an acceptable level.

14.2 Critical thinking and speaking

Task 1 — Walking faster than ever

Pace of life speeds up as study reveals:
  We're walking faster than ever

It is something many of us have long suspected — if only we had time to think about it. The pace of life is speeding up, with stressed-out men and women walking 10 percent faster than just a decade ago.

A secret analysis of pedestrians in more than 30 cities around the world, including London, Edinburgh and Cardiff, revealed that the average pedestrian now speeds along at almost 3.5 mph.

Covering 60 feet on foot now takes just 12.5 seconds — more than a second less than ten years ago.

Experts say the stresses and strains of modern-day life, such as long working hours, coupled with growing reliance on mobile phones, Blackberries, email and fast food, mean we have simply forgotten how to slow down.

They caution that living in a constant rush is bad for our health. Previous research shows those who walk the fastest have a higher than average risk of heart attacks.

It follows a warning that the stress of modern life could spawn an epidemic of heart disease, with high blood pressure blighting the lives of half of adults by 2025.

Working in collaboration with researchers from the British Council, the University of Hertfordshire measured the walking speed of 70 pedestrians in 34 cities around the world.

Men and women were secretly timed between two fixed points as they walked along a city centre street. All of those tracked were walking alone, were not using mobile phones and were unencumbered by heavy bags.

Comparison with results of a similar study carried out in the mid-nineties revealed our walking pace has risen by a tenth.

Psychologist Professor Richard Wiseman, who compiled the research, said, "Some people really thrive on stress but they are few and far between." "The rest of us need to find time to slow down."

"When you speed people up and they become stressed, they don't take care of themselves. They don't eat properly, they don't go to the gym, they start smoking." "With mobile phones and email, you expect almost instant responses." "You email someone and if they don't get back to you in 20 minutes, you think 'What's that about' ."

Prof. Wiseman, who reveals the findings in his new book *Quirkology*（CORR）, added, "The bottom line is that the pace of life is now ten percent faster."

"It can't carry on increasing at the same level. If it did, we would all be running around."

Quickest on their feet were the residents of Singapore, who took just 10.55 seconds to cover 60 feet.

Next fastest were the Danes and Spanish, while Londoners were the 12th speediest walkers, taking 12.17 seconds to walk 60 feet—a speed of 3.36 miles per hour.

The Scots and Welsh were in less of a rush, with residents of Edinburgh taking 13.29 seconds to cover the same distance, while the people of Cardiff took a leisurely 16.81 seconds.

Interestingly, the Irish, often thought of as having a laid-back lifestyle, were among the world's fastest walkers.

Dubliners took the fifth place in the pace of life league, with a time of just 11.03 seconds. The fourth went to Guangzhou, a city in China, with 10.92 seconds.

Most relaxed were the people of Malawi, who by walking at a third of the pace of the speedy Singaporeans, took more than half a minute to complete the task.

Overall, walking speeds had gone up by 10 percent, rising from an average of 2.97 mph to 3.27 mph.

Signs that you may need to slow down include a sense of frustration when stuck behind slower people, when walking along the street and walking out of restaurants and shops, when faced with even a short queue.

Tips for de-stressing include making time for friends and family, exercising and simply trying not to worry.

The Daily Mail's sister paper *the Evening Standard* carried out its own experiment using a pedometer in Hyde Park and found at least one pedestrian travelling well above the London average.

TV producer James Dehaviland（left）managed to cover 60 feet in 10.54 seconds. He attributed his pace to a busy schedule. But others in the park were taking it a bit easier.

Christabel Lawson-Johnson（right）, 26, clocked in at 14.45 seconds. "I tend to dawdle most of the time," she said.

Professor Wiseman said, "Surprisingly, London ranked outside the top 10, suggesting that many in the capital live at a quite healthy pace of life, compared with Copenhagen and Madrid which proved to be the fastest European cities. Madrid, which took the third place with 10.89 seconds, is only to Copenhagen with a time of 10.82 seconds."

Professor Wiseman, whose new book *Quirkology* looks at the psychology of everyday life, said , "People tend to walk more slowly in countries where there is a slower pace of life."

Cultural notes

Edinburgh: the capital of Scotland, 爱丁堡
Cardiff: the capital and largest city of Welsh, 加的夫
University of Hertfordshire: the UK's leading business-facing university, 赫特福德大学,《2015年完全大学指南》该校排名为全英第60名
Dane: a native or inhabitant of Denmark, 丹麦人
Londoner: a resident of London, 伦敦人
Scot: a native or inhabitant of Scotland, 苏格兰人
Welsh: people of Wales, 威尔士人
Irish: people of Ireland, or of the Republic of Ireland, 爱尔兰人
Dubliner: a resident of Dublin which is the capital and major port of the Irish Free State, 都柏林（爱尔兰首都）人
Malawi: a landlocked republic in southeast Africa, 马拉维（非洲国家）
Copenhagen: the capital city and largest city of Denmark, 哥本哈根
Madrid: the capital and largest city situated centrally in Spain, 马德里
1 feet: 12 inches or 30.48 cm

Module 14 City Life

1. Read the passage above and match the words on the left with the correct meanings on the right.

Words		Definition
(1) spawn	A.	to enjoy or be successful in a particular situation, especially one that other people find difficult or unpleasant
(2) blight	B.	damages and spoils
(3) unencumber	C.	do something that helps one to relax
(4) thrive (on)	D.	cause something to happen or to be created
(5) laid-back	E.	prevents one from moving freely or doing what one wants
(6) de-stress	F.	relaxed and seeming not to be worried about anything
(7) dawdle	G.	spend more time than is necessary when going somewhere

2. Scan the passage again and complete the table with the names of cities, time taken to cover 60 feet and the rank.

City or country	0-60 feet in seconds	Rank
		1
	10.82	
	10.89	
Guangzhou		
		5
London		12
	13.29	
Cardiff		
	more than 30	/

233

Pair work

Work with your partner and answer the following questions in turn. Then write down your answers.

(1) How much faster are people walking compared with a decade ago?
_____

(2) What makes people forget how to slow down?
_____

(3) What does the research reveal about people walking faster?
_____

(4) What is the warning about the pressure of modern life?
_____

(5) What are your signs of slowing down?
_____

(6) What can people do to release their stress?
_____

Task 2

After you read the passage, you will be given 10 statements. Each statement describes one of the 10 cities. Read carefully and fill in the gap in front of each statement with the name of the city.

Top 10 livable cities in China in 2013

The latest China Urban Competitiveness Ranking was released by the Hong Kong-based China Institute of City Competitiveness（CICC）in June 2013. The eastern coastal city of Weihai was named the most livable city across the country, according to this year's list.

Zhuhai, a city in Guangdong Province, and Jinhua, a city in Zhejiang Province, respectively ranked second and third in the 2013 ranking.

The list ranks Chinese cities for their living conditions including local governance, public order, environment, economy and culture.

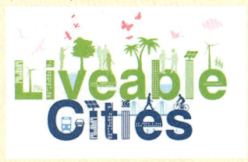

Top 10：Hong Kong（香港）
Score: 73.45

As the "Pearl of the Orient", Hong Kong is a leading financial, banking, trade and tourism center in Asia and the world. Situated off the southeast coast of China, enclosed by the Pearl River Delta and the South China Sea, Hong Kong is renowned for its impressive natural scenery and splendid man-made wonders.

Top 9：Qujing, Yunnan（云南曲靖）
Score: 74.78

Located in the eastern Yunnan Province of Southwest China, Qujing is bordered by Guizhou and Guangxi provinces in the east, and about 135 kilometers west from the provincial capital Kunming. With a favorable climate and a healthy economic growth, Qujing was named as one of the most livable cities in China in 2005, 2006, 2008 and 2012.

Top 8：Quzhou, Zhejiang（浙江衢州）

Score: 75.77

Situated in the west of Zhejiang Province, Quzhou connects Fujian, Jiangxi, Anhui and Zhejiang provinces. Lying in the upper reaches of the Qiantang River, the city features four distinct seasons and a comfortable environment. With over 1,800 years of history, Quzhou was named as one of the National Historical and Cultural Cities of China by the State Council in 1994.

Top 7：Nanning, Guangxi（广西南宁）

Score: 76.68

Settled in the center of Guangxi Zhuang Autonomous Region, Nanning is considered a commercial and communication center, connecting China and Southeast Asia. The pleasant climate endows the city with evergreen trees and fragrant flowers all year round. The city is also home to more than 30 ethnic minority groups, who have been living harmoniously for 1,680 years.

Top 6：Xinyang, Henan（河南信阳）

Score: 77.89

Xinyang, in southern Henan Province, sits between the north foot of Dabie Mountain and the upper reaches of the Huaihe River. At the origins of Chinese civilization, the city embraces a history of more than 8,000 years. With a beautiful landscape and comfortable living condition, Xinyang has consecutively been on the country's Livable City Ranking since 2009.

Top 5：Taichung, Taiwan（台湾台中）

Score: 79.63

Located in Taiwan, Taichung is the third largest city on the island in terms of population, after Taipei and Kaohsiung. With the Taiwan Strait in the west and the Central Mountain Range in the east, the city features splendid mountains, tranquil lakes, beautiful wetlands and fantastic downtown sceneries.

Top 4：Huizhou, Guangdong（广东惠州）

Score: 82.82

Located in the southeast of Guangdong Province, Huizhou is neighbor to Shenzhen and Hong Kong. Settled between Dayawan Bay of the South China Sea and Luofu Mountain, the local scenic areas are varied—mountains, rivers, sea and forests. Huizhou is the headquarter of many famous Chinese enterprises, especially electronics and IT companies, including TCL, Desay Corp., and Huayang General Electronic.

Top 3：Jinhua, Zhejiang（浙江金华）

Score: 83.15

Jinhua is situated in the central part of Zhejiang Province, with Quzhou in the west and Shaoxing and Hangzhou in the north. Featuring a charming landscape and a rich cultural heritage, the city was named as one of the National Historical and Cultural Cities of China by the State Council in 2007. In 2006, 2007, 2008, 2011 and 2012, Jinhua was included in the Top 10 Livable City Ranking.

Top 2：Zhuhai, Guangdong（广东珠海）

Score: 83.56

Lying at the southwest tip of the Pearl River Delta in Guangdong Province, Zhuhai is one of the five Special Economic Zones in China, and a neighbor of Hong Kong and Macau. Consisting of 146 islets, the city is called "City of Islands" and "City of Romance". In recent years, Zhuhai has experienced an impressive economic growth, especially in the electronics, garment and home appliances industries.

Top 1：Weihai, Shandong （山东威海）

Score: 85.23

Weihai, situated in the easternmost part of Shandong Province, is surrounded by the Yellow Sea in the north, east and south. Enjoying a temperate continental monsoon climate, the city has no chilly winter and sweltering summer. In October 6, 2003, Weihai became the first city in China to receive the Habitat Scroll of Honor Award issued by the United Nations.

(1) _____	Apart from being the "City of Romance", it has been undergoing a rapid economic development in garment and electronics industry.
(2) _____	It was named as one of the Most Livable Cities in China in 2005, 2006, 2008 and 2012 with a favorable climate and a healthy economic growth.
(3) _____	With its pleasant climate, it has evergreen trees and fragrant flowers all year round where over 30 ethnic minority groups lived harmoniously for more than ten and a half century.
(4) _____	Its distinguishing feature is its diversified landscape, such as mountains, lakes, wetlands and downtown sceneries.
(5) _____	Known as the "Pearl of the Orient", it is a major global trade hub, financial centre and tourism destination in both Asia and the world.
(6) _____	It is the first city in China to win the Habitat Scroll of Honor Award issued by the United Nations in 2003.
(7) _____	It is known not only for its various scenic areas but also as the base of many famous Chinese electronics and IT companies.
(8) _____	Characterized by both its landscape and cultural heritage, it was named the National Historical and Cultural Cities of China in 2007.
(9) _____	Featuring a long history, beautiful landscape and comfortable living condition, it has consecutively been on the country's Livable City Ranking since 2009.
(10) _____	It is characterized by four distinct seasons and a comfortable environment. It was named as one of the National Historical and Cultural Cities of China in 1994.

Pair work	**Work in pairs and discuss the following questions.**

（1）Which of the top 10 livable cities is your favorite? Why?

（2）Which city do you think would be the best to live in? Why?

（3）If you were the city mayor, what changes would you make to your city to make it more livable?

（4）Do you think there'll be more and more cities in the world? Why or why not?

（5）How do you think city will change in the future?

Assignment

Role-play	**My Typical Day**

You will work in groups of four students. Imagine you are friends who work in different cities, namely Hong Kong, Chengdu, Lijiang and Shanghai. You will talk about your typical day living in your own cities. You should cover the following points in your talk:

（1）housing;

（2）food;

（3）transportation;

（4）work;

（5）entertainment;

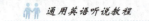

Self-assessment

Review the content covered in this module. How well can you do each of the following?

	very well	well	not well
I know how to compare life in cities with life in the country.	○	○	○
I know how to describe different urban lifestyle choices.	○	○	○
I know some possible negative influence of city life.	○	○	○
I know the pace of city life is speeding up.	○	○	○

Module 15　Future

Module 15
Future

"The afternoon knows what the morning never suspected."
— Robert Frost

"I can't take back the past, but I can fight for the future."
— Shannon A. Thompson

"You can't predict the future, but you can plan for it."
— Saji Ijiyemi

What will the life on Earth be like in the distant future?
What scientific and technological advancements will be achieved?
Is your future predictable?
Where do you see yourself in the future? And how will you plan for your future?

15.1 Listening and speaking

15.1.1 The future of the human race

1. Do you agree or disagree? Why?

> （1）In the future, humans will live on other planets.
> （2）The future of the human race will be wonderful and amazing!
> （3）Humans will be more beautiful and healthy, and will live longer in the future.
> （4）Technology will cause many new problems in the future.
> （5）Humans will become extinct in the future.

2. Match the words in Column A with the synonyms in Column B. Use a dictionary if necessary.

	Column A		Column B
（1）	potboiler	A.	same
（2）	propose	B.	stocky
（3）	homogenous	C.	compassion
（4）	respective	D.	particular
（5）	crutch	E.	decay
（6）	empathy	F.	healthy
（7）	robust	G.	stereotype
（8）	degrade	H.	poor
（9）	squat	I.	suggest
（10）	inferior	J.	support

Module 15 Future

3. Complete the following sentences with the words listed in Column A in the previous exercise.

（1） The future of the human race sounds more like a sci-fi _____.
（2） Evolutionary theorist Oliver Curry _____ that we will evolve into two separate and distinct species.
（3） Increased availability to resources and therapies will bring about a more _____ appearance.
（4） This change will be in the _____ genders.
（5） Technology will affect us for the worse if it becomes a _____ rather than a tool.
（6） People will rely on technology rather than one another, and lose _____ in the process.
（7） Our immune systems won't be as _____ as now.
（8） For the genetically unhealthy, the have-nots, they will continue to _____.
（9） The have-nots will become _____ and ugly.
（10） They will have _____ intelligence,too.

4. Listen to the passage about the future of the human race and check your answers above.

Word tips

hypothesis /haɪˈpɒθəsɪs/ n. 假说，假设
millennium /mɪˈlenɪəm/ n. 一千年，千年
homogenous /ˌhɒməˈdʒiːnɪəs/ adj. 由同类物（人）组成的，同种类的
dodo /ˈdəʊdəʊ/ n. 笨人，蠢人
interbreed /ˌɪntəˈbriːd/ v. （使）杂交繁殖

latte /ˈlɑːteɪ/ n. 热奶沫咖啡，拿铁咖啡
crutch /krʌtʃ/ n. 依靠，依赖
mortality /mɔːˈtæləti/ n. 死亡数量，死亡率
degrade /dɪˈɡreɪd/ v. （使）退化，降解；降低
squat /skwɒt/ adj. 矮而宽的，矮胖的

5. Listen to the passage again and tell whether the following statements are true（T）or false（F）.

（1） Humans will become two different species in the future.   T/F
（2） Rich and poor will divide the species.   T/F
（3） Technology will greatly help us in the future, so we should rely on it.   T/F
（4） According to the passage, medicine will eventually harm the human race.   T/F
（5） People in 100,000 years will more or less have the same intelligence.   T/F

Pair discussion

6. What do you think the two human faces might look like in 100,000 years? Why?

🔊 **7. Listen to the report and fill in the blanks. You will be able to figure out the sketch of their outlooks in the far away future.**

What will humans look like in 100,000 years?

The future is always unknown, especially the (1) _____ future, but that shouldn't stop us from making (2) _____ guesses. That's exactly what artist and researcher Nickolay Lamm did with help from Dr. Alan Kwan, who has a (n) (3) _____ in computational genomics (基因组学) from Washington University. Their (4) _____ point was the question: "What do you think the human face might look like in 100,000 years and why?"

From there, they reasoned out how (5) _____ with advanced genetic engineering technology might (6) _____ itself over time, taking over the role played by natural (7) _____ so far. Lamm then created a series of (8) _____ of what he thinks the human face might look like 20,000 years, 60,000 years and 100,000 years in the future.

In 20,000 years, there may not be too major changes yet. Heads would be a bit (9) _____ to accommodate larger brains, and those yellow rings that you see in the model's eyes are special lenses that act kind of like Google Glass does today, but in a much more powerful way.

In 60,000 years, we're starting to see some (10) _____ changes. Heads would be even (11) _____, but the eyes would have (12) _____ too. Lamm speculates that this would be a result of human (13) _____ of the solar system, with people living farther away from the sun where there is less (14) _____. Skin pigmentation (天然肤色) would change and our eyelids would become (15) _____ to offer more protection against UV rays for those living outside of the earth's (16) _____ ozone layer.

244

100,000 years! Here Lamm predicts big changes, the most (17) _____ of which is the big Japanese Manga-style（日本漫画风格）eyes to offer extra (18) _____ against cosmic rays. These futuristic faces follow the golden ratio proportions and are perfectly symmetrical（对称的）from left to right, and have larger nostrils（鼻孔）to make (19) _____ in off-planet environments easier, as well as (20) _____ hair to contain heat loss from their even larger heads. Various (21) _____ might allow the man and woman of the future to always be connected, but these would be (22) _____ and almost invisible.

Nickolay Lamm and Dr. Kwan stress that this is not a prediction, but rather (23) _____ ("one possible time line"), and that it is impossible to know for sure what the future (24) _____. This is just their answer to the question: "What do you think the human face might look like in 100,000 years and why?" There are, without a doubt, many other answers, some of which might seem more (25) _____. But it's interesting food for thought.

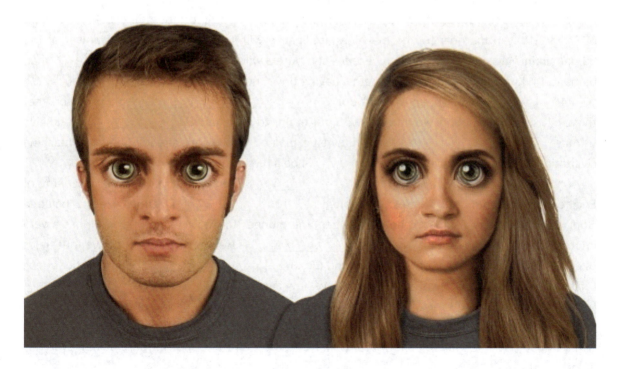

Designer Lamm's depiction of how the human face might look in 100,000 years

15.1.2 Future science and technology

1. Match the following with their synonyms.

（1）	leading	A.	speed
（2）	predicted	B.	point out
（3）	within	C.	future
（4）	upcoming	D.	developer
（5）	extension	E.	top
（6）	identify	F.	specialists
（7）	experts	G.	forecast
（8）	pioneer	H.	inside
（9）	pace	I.	sci-fi
（10）	science fiction	J.	addition

2. Listen to the passage and fill in the missing information.

Computers to match man by 2029

A leading US scientist has predicted that computers will be （1）_____ humans by 2029. Futurologist Dr. Ray Kurzweil told the American Association for the Advancement of Science that in the near future, machine intelligence will （2）_____ the power of the human brain. He said that within two decades computers will be able to think（3）_____ than humans. Dr. Kurzweil painted a picture of us having tiny robots called nanobots（超微型机器人装置）（4）_____ in our brain to boost our（5）_____. He told reporters that these microscopic nanobots would work with our brains to make us （6）_____ and give us more （7）_____. Kurzweil explained that we are already "a human machine civilization" and that the upcoming technology "will be a further （8）_____ of that".

Dr. Kurzweil was one of 18 top （9）_____ asked by the US National Academy of Engineering to identify our greatest technological （10）_____. Other experts included Google founder Larry Page and the human genome pioneer Dr. Craig Venter. Kurzweil has a very impressive background in （11）_____. He was an innovator in various fields of computing, including the technology behind CDs. He also（12）_____ automatic speech recognition by machines. He predicts the pace of new inventions will （13）_____ from now, saying, "… the next half century will see （14）_____ times more technical progress than the past half century." This means scenes from （15）_____ movies, like *Blade Runner*, *The Terminator* and *I Robot*, will become more and more a part of our everyday lives.

15.1.3 Future telling

1. Work in pairs and discuss the following questions with your partner.

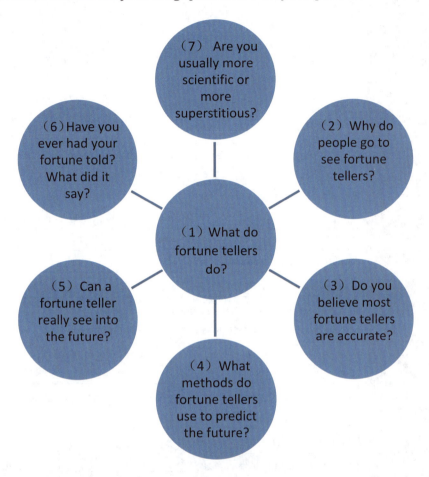

(1) What do fortune tellers do?
(2) Why do people go to see fortune tellers?
(3) Do you believe most fortune tellers are accurate?
(4) What methods do fortune tellers use to predict the future?
(5) Can a fortune teller really see into the future?
(6) Have you ever had your fortune told? What did it say?
(7) Are you usually more scientific or more superstitious?

2. Listen to the passage about fortune telling and fill in the missing information.

Definition of fortune telling	the practice of (1) _____ the future, usually of an individual, through (2) _____ or (3) _____ means	
Common methods used	astrology	
	tarot card reading	
	crystallomancy	
	palmistry	interpreting the (4) _____ of the hand and the (5) _____ of the palm to determine your (6) _____ and life experiences
		Type 1: to tell your future by reading the lines on the (7) _____ of your hand
		Type 2: to read the strengths and weaknesses of your (8) _____ from the shape of your hand
Other forms of fortune telling	the observation of the wind (9) _____ and cloud formation	
	interpreting the (10) _____ when a hatchet is smacked into a table	
	reading (11) _____, tea leaves or coffee grinds	
	reading the holes or mold in (12) _____	
	interpreting the lines in your (13) _____ button	
What is a psychic?	someone who claims to have paranormal or (14) _____ powers that he or she uses to answer your questions or make observations about you	
Props or aids a psychic uses	tarot cards, astrological charts, your palm, or pieces of jewelry or metal that have been (15) _____ your skin	
Issues psychic reading can focus on	issues of the past, present or future and are offered in various degrees of (16) _____	
Visiting a psychic	How much of it you take seriously is up to (17) _____.	
How do most people view fortune tellers?	They see fortune tellers as (18) _____, rather than actually predicting what will happen in the future.	

3. Brainstorming.

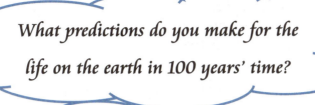

What predictions do you make for the life on the earth in 100 years' time?

e.g.:
（1）Oceans will be extensively farmed and not just for fish.
（2）We will have the ability to communicate through thought transmission.
（3）Thanks to DNA and robotic engineering, we will have created incredibly intelligent humans who are immortal.
（4）There will only be three languages in the world—English, Spanish and Mandarin.
  ...

15.1.4 Future planning

Planning for the future is an important step to ensure your future happiness and success. It is about taking responsibility for yourself and your actions.

1. Work in groups to develop more ideas on how to build your future.

(1) Secure your future financially.
e.g.: Open a savings account and decide on savings goals.
1) ...
2) ...
3) ...

(2) Secure your future professionally.
e.g.: Write yourself detailed and achievable career goals for yourself in 1 year, 5 years, 10 years.
1) ...
2) ...
3) ...

(3) Secure your future socially.
e.g.: Value your relationships with friends and family.
1) ...
2) ...
3) ...

(4) Secure your future personally.
e.g.: Invest time in hobbies you enjoy.
1) ...
2) ...
3) ...

Module 15 Future

🔊 **2. Listen to the passage about how to prepare for a future career and complete the table below.**

Brainstorm about occupations that（1）_____ you.	Think about questions like: a. Would you like to work with many other people or（2）_____? b. Would you prefer to work in an office or（3）_____? c. Does（4）_____ matter to you? d. Would you rather pursue dreams that may be less financially（5）_____? Suggestions: Use a（6）_____ test to determine which careers match you.
Find out how much（7）_____ is typically required for a career you are interested in.	For example: a. A registered nurse may need anywhere from a high school diploma to a（8）_____ degree in nursing. b. A postsecondary teacher may need a（9）_____ to even be considered for a job.
Determine what kind of（10）_____ or additional（11）_____ you'll need for a particular career.	The importance of experience in a particular field（12）_____. a. You may be able to（13）_____ or obtain an internship in a certain industry. b. You may be able to work as an（14）_____ or be mentored by a professional.
Hone any（15）_____ that are necessary for success in your industry.	Visit your library to find books about your industry, and read others'（16）_____ to see how they prepared for their careers.
Talk to（17）_____ in your field of interest.	You can meet them at conferences, career（18）____ or even on location where they work. You may also be able to contact some professionals through email or（19）_____. It may help to ask them what（20）_____ parts about their job are, how they got started in their careers and what they would have done（21）_____.

15.2 Critical thinking and speaking

Task 1

Studying the future

Believe it or not, but there are people who study the future. They don't use magic. They don't have special abilities to see into the future. They don't just guess. These people look at the past and the present, then try to determine possible, probable, and preferable futures for humankind. They are called "futurists".

There are many important topics that futurists try to understand. They look at the challenges humans face on our planet today, and ask questions about tomorrow. For example:

- How can everyone have clean water in the future?
- How can global communication help everyone?
- How can we safely increase energy production?
- How can we balance limited resources and population growth in the future?

But futurists also want to understand how new developments will change society. They look at trends, discoveries, and developments in computers, energy, leisure, medicine, politics, robots, and space.

Their ideas may seem like science fiction. For example, there will be intelligent robots in every house by 2020 and a colony on the Mars by 2025. In fact, these ideas may even seem unimportant, especially when there are more serious problems in the world today. But futurists believe that all of these ideas are important because they will affect everyday life in the future. For example, how would society change if every house had a robot to cook and clean? Would that affect leisure time? Would that affect how children are raised? Would that affect people's work habits? These questions are as important as other questions that focus on clean water, pollution, or energy production.

Humankind needs to know what could happen in the future, or so the futurists believe. The world changes very quickly now. People's attitudes and values are also changing quickly. Additionally, these changes are coming at a faster and faster pace. It's important to understand what lies ahead, so it then becomes easier to make the right decisions and take action now. It's important to understand that the choices we make today will have consequences for our children and our children's children.

Futurists believe that there are desirable futures and undesirable futures. We need to work towards the best one together.

Discuss the following questions with your partner:

(1) What is a futurist?

(2) What is the difference between being a futurist and a fortune teller?

(3) What do the futurists concern about?

(4) Why do the futurists think the birth of intelligent robots is a topic as important as clean water, pollution or energy production?

(5) In what way do you think the endeavor of the futurists is worthwhile?

Module 15 Future

Task 2   *Would you take a one-way trip to the Mars?*

Step right up and prove why you should get a one-way ticket to the Mars! Well, wait — you might want to know a little more about the venture first.

A Dutch company called Mars One began looking Monday for volunteer astronauts to fly to the Mars. Departure for the Red Planet is scheduled for 2022, landing seven months later in 2023. The space travelers will return ... never. They will finish out their lives on the Mars, representatives from the non-profit said. "It's likely that there will be a crematorium（火葬场）," said CEO Bas Lansdorp. "It's up to the people on the Mars to decide what to do with their death." Still, the company said it has received more than 10,000 e-mails from interested would-be spacefarers.

The one-way ticket makes the mission possible because it greatly reduces costs, and the technology for a return flight doesn't exist, according to Mars One's website. At a news conference, Lansdorp maintained that "no new inventions are needed to land humans on the Mars."

NASA: Yes, Mars could have hosted life

The biggest obstacles, he said, are financial. The company has revealed some of its sponsors and hopes to gain more via media coverage. It's not clear whether enough money will be collected in time.

There are also practical issues: Can the kinks（奇想）in having a sustainable system for people to survive in such a harsh environment be worked out by 2023? "Questions of reliability and robustness have to be answered before we leave the Earth," said Grant Anderson of Paragon Space Development Corporation, which builds life-support systems and is joining the Mars One effort.

Strange, dangerous mission

As far as getting to the Mars, Lansdorp said his organization is in discussions with SpaceX, the company that has now completed two commercial cargo missions to the International Space Station. The idea would be to use a slightly enlarged version of the Dragon capsule and land with retro-propulsion（火箭推进装置）, not by parachute（降落伞）.

If they get there, Mars astronauts will face a lonely life of danger, subsisting for extended periods on dried and canned food. They will get some of their water by recycling their urine（尿液）.

They will have to take care of sickness and injuries themselves. "There will be emergencies and deaths," Lansdorp said. "We need to make

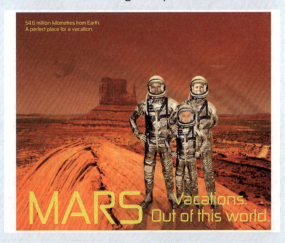

sure that crew members can continue without those people." Mars astronauts will have to be mentally fit to deal with the unusual stresses, he said. "Their psychological skills will be the main selection criteria we will use," he said. Once selected, a group of 40 astronauts will undergo seven years of training.

The flight to the Earth's neighbor, with its barren（贫瘠的）red desert landscape and thin carbon dioxide atmosphere, sounds almost worse than a lifetime on it. The crew of four will be cooped up on a rocket for seven months with a limited supply of food and water. It also might smell bad. "Showering with water will not be an option" on the journey there, according to Mars One's website.

DO YOU WANT TO APPLY?

- Candidates must:
  be at least 18 years of age;
  have a deep sense of purpose, willingness to build and maintain healthy relationships, the capacity for self-reflection and ability to trust;
- Candidates will receive a minimum of eight years extensive training while employed by Mars One;
- Any formal education or real-world experience can be an asset; all skills required on the Mars will be learned while in training.

* Mars One says it is not necessary to have military training nor experience in flying aircraft nor even a science degree.

Assignment

Please prepare a 2-minute-long oral report on your answers to this question and give your reasons.

About Mars One

Mars One is a not-for-profit foundation that will establish a permanent human settlement on the Mars. Human settlement on the Mars is possible today with existing technologies. Mars One's mission plan integrates components that are well tested and readily available from industry leaders worldwide. The first footprint on the Mars and lives of the crew thereon will captivate and inspire generations; it is this public interest that will help finance this human mission to the Mars.

Self-assessment

Review the content covered in this module. How well can you do each of the following?

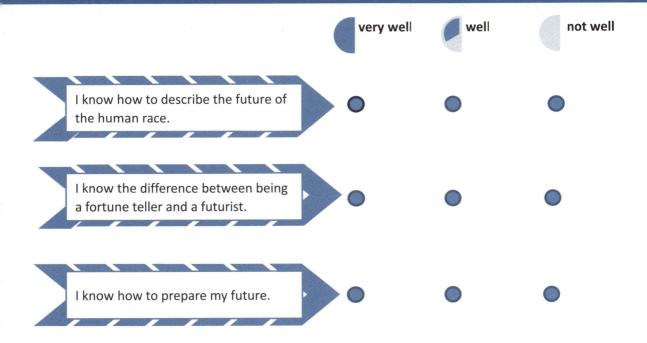

	very well	well	not well
I know how to describe the future of the human race.	○	○	○
I know the difference between being a fortune teller and a futurist.	○	○	○
I know how to prepare my future.	○	○	○